Unapologetically You

Reflections on Life & the Human Experience

Steve Maraboli

Unapologetically You

Reflections on Life & the Human Experience

A Better Today Publishing

P.O. Box 1433
Port Washington, NY 11050

www.abettertodaypublishing.com

A Better Today Publishing
P.O. Box 1433
Port Washington, NY 11050

www.abettertodaypublishing.com

Cover design by: Chamillah Designs
www.chamillah.com

ISBN 13: 978-0-9795750-8-2
ISBN 10: 0-9795750-8-7

Dedicated to my mom and dad:
Thank you for having the courage to raise me right.

To my family and friends:
Thank you for your support and love.

To my readers, viewers, and listeners: See above; I consider you my family & friends.

I love you all!

Table of Contents

Inspiration & Motivation...

Dreams & Goals...

Life & Happiness...

Love & Relationships...

God & Spirituality...

Introduction:

Hi everyone!

Thank you for taking the time to read this book. I am honored that my insights, musings, ramblings, and observations have captured the attention of so many people. The intent for sharing my words is to inspire you to live your greatest life. I don't write books so that you can become fascinated with me; I write them so you can become fascinated with you.

This book contains more of my written work and spoken ideas that were gathered from my speeches, blogs, radio shows, and social media posts. Like the work from my first book, "Life, the Truth, and Being Free", the pieces and quotes in this book have been posted and published all over the world. Having my words touch so many lives is an honor I can't even describe. Thank you!

As usual, I don't overly concern myself with grammatical rules, but on the effectiveness of delivering the intended message. I am not a long-winded philosopher; I like to convey my ideas and strategies with accuracy and practicality.

This book is divided into five sections:

Inspiration & Motivation
Dreams & Goals
Life & Happiness
Love & Relationships
God & Spirituality

Each section has many pages of my popular quotes as well as written pieces dedicated to the topic. As with my other books, this book is designed to be opened to any page. Within the pages of this book you will find a plethora of practical wisdom, strategies for success, recipes for happiness, reflections on life, powerful ideas, and much more. You will even find "Notes to my Younger Self" sprinkled throughout the pages. These are things I wish I knew then... but I'm glad I know now. In short, this book is my mind, heart, and soul put to paper.

From sharing my first book in 1999 to sharing this one, I feel very blessed to have matured in my thinking and to have connected with some amazing friends along this great journey.

Thank you all for buying this book and for sharing my words. Let the ideas within these pages inspire you to take action... action that will shape the life you wish to live.

Enjoy!

-       Steve

Inspiration

&

Motivation...

Empty Your Cup

One of my favorite stories concerns famed martial artist, Bruce Lee, and his desire to be trained by a local Master. At the time, Bruce had extensive fight experience and a background in martial arts training. He approached the Master, and after making the customary bows, asked him to be his teacher.

At that time, Bruce began to talk about his experience and rambled on and on about the many fights he had won. The Master listened patiently and then began to make tea. When it was ready, he poured the tea into Bruce's cup. As Bruce watched, the cup slowly filled until it began to overflow, first on to the table and then on to the floor. While trying to be respectful Bruce couldn't hold it in any longer and shouted, "Stop, stop! The cup is full; you can't get any more in."

The master stopped pouring and said, "You are like this cup; you are full of ideas and opinions. You come and ask for teaching, but your cup is full; I can't put anything in. Before I can teach you, you will have to empty your cup."

This story is an old one that surely has been retold throughout the generations, but it continues to be played out in our day-to-day lives. We are so enamored of our own ideas and opinions, and so trapped by our conditioning that we fill ourselves up to the brim and nothing new can get in. Empty your cup!

Throughout my own life I've noticed that I have had to empty my cup, haven't you? I've noticed that in our own lives we sometimes get in our own way because we think we're experts at something. Because of this, we become judgers instead of analyzers. We become filled with our own ideas, judgments, and opinions that keep us from learning and processing new information.

If you allow it, life can be a very interesting and dynamic process of learning. Life is a journey; it's a process that presents us with new stimulus every single day, new ideas every single day, new occurrences every single day.

If you're in a relationship, there are new dynamics that reveal themselves every single day. The good news is, you have the capacity to experience all of it, or most of it. The bad news is, you very rarely will because your cup is still full of past experiences... Past drama, past labels, past truths, that have rendered you incapable of being open to the new dynamics, the new stimulus of your life and of your journey.

How would your life benefit from emptying your cup right now? Emptying your cup from your past relationships, from your past dramas, from your past betrayals, from your past judgments. Imagine how your life could benefit from this!

Empty your cup! Empty your cup of the idea that you're not in charge of your life. Empty your cup of the idea that you can't change the world around you. Empty your cup of the idea that you are powerless to refine and improve your life. Empty your cup of those habits, ideas, and philosophies that hinder your ability to experience, learn, and enjoy all the new dynamics this journey reveals to you.

ഓരു

You would not be here today if yesterday was your defining moment. LIVE THIS DAY and move towards your dreams.

ഓരു

We may place blame, give reasons, and even have excuses; but in the end, it is an act of cowardice to not follow your dreams.

ഓരു

Everything is easier said than done. Wanting something is easy. Saying something is easy. The challenge and the reward are in the doing.

ഓരു

You're frustrated because you keep waiting for the blooming of flowers of which you have yet to sow the seeds.

ഓരു

Let today be the day you love yourself enough to no longer just dream of a better life; let it be the day you act upon it.

ഓരു

Sometimes life knocks you on your ass... get up, get up, get up!!! Happiness is not the absence of problems; it's the ability to deal with them.

ഓരു

ॐ≪

Stop waiting for the perfect day or the perfect moment... Take THIS day, THIS moment and lead it to perfection.

ॐ≪

To embark on the journey towards your goals and dreams requires bravery. To remain on that path requires courage. The bridge that merges the two is commitment.

ॐ≪

Rise to the challenge of bringing your dreams to life! Do not be discouraged by resistance, be nourished by it. Success is the experience of rising to the level of your true greatness.

ॐ≪

The universe doesn't give you what you ask for with your thoughts; it gives you what you demand with your actions.

ॐ≪

Faith is the poetry of our dreams; action is the builder of our reality.

ॐ≪

Excuses, criticisms, and superstitions are vitamins for haters, but poison for the successful. Rise above!

ॐ≪

Sometimes You Have to Lose to Win

Life sure can hit you hard! Suddenly, when you least expect it, WHAM; life has a knack for challenging you in ways that you don't feel prepared for. I feel like life sometimes tests and shapes you in a manner in which you feel least equipped. It seems you don't get to choose the exercise equipment God challenges and builds your strength with.

When this is happening, it's easy to drop into a victim mindset. It's easy to feel stuck, defeated, and like you are a losing player in the game of life. This victim mindset argues (very loudly) that we have lost; that nothing good is on the horizon. Never forget that the volume of an argument does not reflect the validity of the argument. Just because the victim mentality argues that we are losing, doesn't mean that it's true. In fact, I have come to realize that during the times in my life when I thought I was losing, I was actually winning.

An empowered perspective helps me see that I can only get stronger when working against resistance. It is when I struggle that I strengthen. It is when challenged to my core that I learn the depth of who I am. It is when we feel broken that we can become experts at mending.

I am who I am because the tears of my past have watered the magnificence of my present. It is from my broken hearts that I learned the measure and power of true love. Every job I was denied for... opened the door to new opportunities. Every relationship that hurt me... led me to my true love. Every mistake I thought would be the end of me... pointed me towards an incredible success. Sometimes when you think you're losing, you're winning.

The past will be your

teacher if you learn from it;

your master if you live in it.

୫୦୦ଷ

The successful person and the unsuccessful person are looking at the same world; the difference between them is what they see.

୫୦୦ଷ

My life changed the day I moved beyond just wishing for things and I started earning them. That is the day I learned that we don't get what we wish for, we get what we work for.

୫୦୦ଷ

If you hang out with chickens, you're going to cluck; and if you hang out with eagles, you're going to fly.

୫୦୦ଷ

Protect your enthusiasm from the negativity and fear of others. Never decide to do nothing just because you can only do a little. Do what you can. You would be surprised at what "little" acts have done for our world.

୫୦୦ଷ

The disempowered mind believes dreams come true; the empowered mind knows you bring your dreams to life.

୫୦୦ଷ

Blame is the creed of the disempowered.

୫୦୦ଷ

ॐ

How much longer will you sit back and wait for your dream to spontaneously come true? Too many days, weeks, months, and years have passed! Do not be unresponsive to your own dreams. Now, set a course of action that will lead to bringing your dream into reality.

ॐ

If the self-help books worked, it would be a shrinking industry not a growing one.

ॐ

Take ACTION! When we DO NOT take action, our potentiality becomes the soil that houses the seeds of our regret.

ॐ

Stop just cheering for others who are living their visions. Commit yourself to your own success and follow the steps required to achieve it.

ॐ

Those who have the ability to be grateful are the ones who have the ability to achieve greatness.

ॐ

Be creative and daring in your dreams and the steps you take to bring them to fruition.

ॐ

Notes to my Younger Self

Be the type of friend you would
like to have.

Let Mistakes Be What They Are;
A Gauge

To step into an empowered state of mind is to gain control over the ability to label events in a manner that strengthens our journey instead of weakening it. For the disempowered mindset, ideas cast tremendously scary shadows that tend to cripple one's movement towards success. One of these crippling ideas is the big scary monster often referred to as a "mistake."

Sometimes we don't take action towards our goals because we are afraid to make a mistake. Mistakes aren't something to be afraid of. They can be helpful in our quest towards our goals and dreams. Don't think of them as a reflection of failure; think of them as a scientific result of your current methods. If we don't take mistakes so personally, they can serve as a guide for how to improve our process.

You express the truth of your character with the choice of your actions.

৪০০৪

When people tell me they can't afford to join a gym, I tell them to go outside; planet Earth is a gym and we're already members. Run, climb, sweat, and enjoy all of the natural wonder that is available to you.

৪০০৪

This magical universe is so faithful in waiting for us to get out of our own way. No matter how long you have gone astray, when you take action, the universe moves to support the act. Move in the direction of your goals and watch the magic flow.

৪০০৪

Dream your dream; and realize that you are more than just the dreamer; you are the point of origin for its reality.

৪০০৪

When you are just EXISTING, life happens to you... and you manage; when you are truly LIVING, you happen to life... and you lead.

৪০০৪

Take action! An inch of movement will bring you closer to your goals than a mile of intention.

৪০০৪

The strong-minded rise to the challenge of their goals and dreams. The weak-minded become haters.

৪০০৪

ഇൽ

Act upon your goals! Ask yourself, "If somebody was watching my day to day behavior and actions, would they be able to see what I'm working towards; what my goals are?" If the answer is no, FIX IT!

ഇൽ

Your life is a reflection... you don't get what you WANT, you get what you ARE. You gotta BE it to SEE it.

ഇൽ

Anyone who ever bet against you was wrong. Don't let their opinion blind you from your reality. You were not meant to live their life; live yours!

ഇൽ

No Blame: The most liberating and empowering day of my life was the day I freed myself from my own self-destructive nonsense.

ഇൽ

When we replace a sense of service and gratitude with a sense of entitlement and expectation, we quickly see the demise of our relationships, society, and economy.

ഇൽ

Don't limit yourself to someone else's opinion of your capabilities. Be you. Dream, plan, execute!

ഇൽ

On the Other Side of Challenges

There are times when life seems to unmercifully pile-on the challenges. It is very frustrating! I have been there too many times to count. However, as I look back, I recognize those trying times as my greatest moments of personal growth.

Along this journey of life, I have learned that even though the challenge is great, so is the reward. It's a long life, and rough times are plentiful. When you are going through a rough patch of life, don't EVER forget that a GREAT life is waiting for you at the other end of those trying days.

While most people fear those challenging times, it is those very moments in life that will define who we are and what kind of life we will have. Always remember that you are greater than all of these challenges; rise above, reach your greatest potential, and experience the great life it has earned you.

> *Life is simple, it's just not easy.*

෩෨

This is not the time to be passive. This is the time to shape, sculpt, paint, participate... the time to get sweaty, to get dirty, to fall in love, to forgive, to forget, to hug, to refresh, to kiss... this is the time to experience, participate, and live your life as a verb.

෩෨

Set the standard! Stop expecting others to show you love, acceptance, commitment, and respect when you don't even show that to yourself.

෩෨

The healthy life: It's not just about losing the weight; it's about losing the lifestyle and mindset that got you there.

෩෨

BREAKING NEWS: You're awesome and designed for success; live this day accordingly!

෩෨

Sometimes the greatest thing to come out of all your hard work isn't what you GET for it, but what you BECOME for it.

෩෨

Stop lying to yourself. When we deny our own truth, we deny our own potential.

෩෨

৪০৫৪

Live Today! Do not allow your spirit to be softened or your happiness to be limited by a day you cannot have back or a day that does not yet exist.

৪০৫৪

Be driven with purpose. Be relentless in your alignment with excellence. Pay no mind to the disimpassioned impotent haters.

৪০৫৪

The beautiful journey of today can only begin when we learn to let go of yesterday.

৪০৫৪

It's time to care; it's time to take responsibility; it's time to lead; it's time for a change; it's time to be true to our greatest self; it's time to stop blaming others.

৪০৫৪

Make a pact with yourself today to not be defined by your past. Instead, shake things up today! Live through today. Don't just exist through it - LIVE through it!

৪০৫৪

Learn from the past, but don't live in the past.

৪০৫৪

Notes to my Younger Self

Most people will talk the talk,
few will walk the walk; be
amongst those few.

The Observer Test

What would someone watching think?

Think about what your actions tell the people around you. Based on your behavior, would the people around you be surprised to hear about your goals and dreams? A person's behavior has always been a more effective and convincing communicator than their words.

Efficiency in journeying towards success and excellence is sculpted when your empty words are chiseled away by your purpose-driven action. No more impotent resolutions! Stop throwing away days, weeks, months, and years by simply day-dreaming about what you wish your life would be.

Pay attention to the message your actions are speaking. If there is a disconnect between what you want and what your actions are speaking, make the adjustment. When your actions are aligned with your dreams and goals, you become the point of origin for their reality.

꧁ꩦ

Renew, release, let go. Yesterday's gone. There's nothing you can do to bring it back. You can't "should've" done something. You can only DO something. Renew yourself. Release that attachment. Today is a new day!

꧁ꩦ

This moment is yours and yours alone! Take charge, seize this moment and allow it to propel you to the high levels of an empowered life. Allow upon this fertile moment to be planted the seeds of your happiness and success.

꧁ꩦ

The new day has greeted us with no rules except for the rules we placed with it, greet it with open arms and endless possibility.

꧁ꩦ

Your actions must reflect your goals in order to experience true success. Don't just wish, DO! Don't just dream, BE! Let today be the day you create a plan and follow it.

꧁ꩦ

Don't let the agony, regret, or fog of yesterday blind you to the fact that each new day carries with it a plethora of opportunities to move your life into the right direction.

꧁ꩦ

෨෨ඐ

Free yourself from the poisonous and laborious burden of holding a grudge. When you hold a grudge, you want someone else's sorrow to reflect your level of hurt, but the two rarely meet. Let go... Sometimes, forgiveness is simply a reflection of loving yourself enough to move on.

෨෨ඐ

Live your truth. Express your love. Share your enthusiasm. Take action towards your dreams. Walk your talk. Dance and sing to your music. Embrace your blessings. Make today worth remembering.

෨෨ඐ

Each day brings a fresh opportunity for you to set the standard of how dedicated and committed you are to your needs, wants, goals, and relationships.

෨෨ඐ

You gotta be in the NOW to create and experience the WOW!

෨෨ඐ

If you fuel your journey on the opinions of others, you are going to run out of gas.

෨෨ඐ

Let your words merely reiterate what your actions have already stated.

෨෨ඐ

A Life Well Lived

Many people experience the travesty of regret in their end days; the realization that nothing held them back, that nothing was in their way, that there is no one to blame, only themselves.

What are you waiting for?

Don't just sit by waiting for your life to happen, make it happen! Don't just hope your dreams will come alive, breathe life into them! Don't let your fear help you birth a well-nourished regret; take action today!

Be amongst the few who dare to follow their dreams!

Cemeteries are full of unfulfilled dreams... countless echoes of "could have" and "should have"... countless books unwritten... countless songs unsung...

Don't choose to walk the well-worn path to regret. Live your life in such a way that when your body is laid to rest, it will be a well needed rest from a life well lived, a song well sung, a book well written, opportunities well explored, and a love well expressed.

There will always be fear; do it anyway. Let your courage inspire the world around you!

Nobody ever talks about the pyramids that weren't built... the books that weren't written... the songs that weren't sung...

Stop letting your fear condemn you to mediocrity. Get out of your own way. Your dreams are a poetic reflection of your soul's wishes. Be courageous enough to follow them. There is no greater time than now to experience the full power of your potential. Make this the day you take the first step in the beautiful journey of bringing your dreams to life.

Today is a new day. This is your chance; your moment. Dare to exhaust yourself with all the opportunities this day offers along the path to your dreams.

Live courageously bold! Live in such a manner that at the end of this day, at the end of this year, at the end of this precious life, you can hold your head up high, smile, and be proud of a life well lived.

There is great change to be experienced once you learn the power of letting go.
Stop allowing anyone or anything control, limit, repress, or discourage you from being your true self! Today is YOURS to shape – own it – break free from people and things that poison or dilute your spirit.

ഓരു

A new day: Be open enough to see opportunities. Be wise enough to be grateful. Be courageous enough to be happy.

ഓരു

You will find that people will always have opinions about your decisions. Don't take it personally, it's simply because they're not courageous enough to take action in their own lives. Be a leader in your life and pay no mind to those who lack the courage to do the same in theirs.

ഓരു

Stop walking through the motions of a conditioned routine and start consciously taking action on your visualized intent.

ഓരു

You have a unique gift to offer this world. Be true to yourself, be kind to yourself, read and learn about everything that interests you, and keep away from people who bring you down. When you treat yourself kindly and respect the uniqueness of those around you, you will be giving this world an amazing gift...
YOU!

ഓരു

It's not about having an absence of fear, it's about having dominance over it.

ഓരു

ജ്ഞ

Don't keep all your feelings sheltered - express them. Don't EVER let life shut you up.

ജ്ഞ

When you are living the best version of yourself, you inspire others to live the best versions of themselves.

ജ്ഞ

People tend to be generous when sharing their nonsense, fear, and ignorance. And while they seem quite eager to feed you their negativity, please remember that sometimes the diet we need to be on is a spiritual and emotional one. Be cautious with what you feed your mind and soul. Fuel yourself with positivity and let that fuel propel you into positive action.

ജ്ഞ

The victim mindset dilutes the human potential. By not accepting personal responsibility for our circumstances, we greatly reduce our power to change them.

ജ്ഞ

Start shaping your own day. Start walking your own walk. This journey is yours, take charge of it. Stop giving other people the power to shape your life.

ജ്ഞ

Notes to my Younger Self

The people who claim to be

the most spiritual are usually

the least so.

Jumpstart

I love reminding people of the greatness they have within. Sometimes it feels like I have performed a spiritual and emotional jumpstart.

While in the military, I was stationed in North Dakota. The landscape was beautiful and the people were kind, but the winter weather was very, very cold. The unforgiving cold led to a common situation of seeing cars in need of a jumpstart.

When I would see someone on the side of the road or in a parking lot with a dead battery, I would pull up next to them and take out my jumper cables and by attaching my living battery to their dead one, they were able to start their car.

During that process, my functioning battery doesn't have to teach their dead battery how to be a battery. The process of jumpstarting doesn't teach the battery to be what it already is. All the living battery does is remind the dead battery of its initial potential. It reminds it of its power. Once the dead battery is back to functioning within its potential, I disconnect my cables and wave good-bye as they drive away.

When people send me emails, or speak to me after my seminars, and thank me for teaching them to be amazing or successful, I think of this jumpstart scenario. I don't teach you how to be amazing; you're already amazing. I don't teach you to be resilient; you are already resilient. I don't teach you to be successful; you are already designed for success. What I do, along this journey of life, is stop along the way when I encounter someone whose journey has ceased, and connect with them to jumpstart and remind them of the greatness within.

Keep in mind that you too will come across people who need a spiritual or emotional jumpstart. Connect with these individuals and remind them of their potentiality, of their beauty, of their worth, and of their innate strength... then let them be on their way, so that they may do the same for someone else.

> *Nobody ever talks about the pyramids that weren't built, the books that weren't written, the songs that weren't sung. Stop letting your fear condemn you to mediocrity. Get out of your own way, your dreams are a poetic reflection of your soul's wishes. Be courageous enough to follow them. There is no greater time than now to experience the full power of your potential. Make this the day you take the first step in the beautiful journey of bringing your dreams to life.*

৪৩৫৯

If people refuse to look at you in a new light and they can only see you for what you were, only see you for the mistakes you've made, if they don't realize that you are not your mistakes, then they have to go.

৪৩৫৯

Every new day is a once in a lifetime event. Think of how much more exciting our lives would be if we embraced this truth and lived accordingly!

৪৩৫৯

When used as a tool, fear will enhance your preparedness; when used as a guide, it will stop your progress.

৪৩৫৯

Don't be so quick to count out the teenagers. Some of the world's greatest changes, brilliant poetry, and amazing innovations have come from the teenage mind.

৪৩৫৯

Let today be the day that you become committed in being, in doing, in getting, in achieving, in experiencing. Let today be the day that you are committed to being the change you wish to see and living the life you wish to live.

৪৩৫৯

৪০৫৪

Do not dilute the truth of your potential. We often convince ourselves that we cannot change, that we cannot overcome the circumstances of our lives. That is simply not true. You have been blessed with immeasurable power to make positive changes in your life. But you can't just wish it, you can't just hope it, you can't just want it... you have to LIVE it, BE it, DO it.

৪০৫৪

Your complaints, your drama, your victim mentality, your whining, your blaming, and all of your excuses have NEVER gotten you even a single step closer to your goals or dreams. Let go of your nonsense. Let go of the delusion that you DESERVE better and go EARN it!

৪০৫৪

Stop living within the confines of how others define you! You weren't created to live their life; you were created to live yours - so LIVE it! You can reignite that fire within and bring the passion back into your goals, dreams, ambitions, careers, and relationships by reclaiming control of your own life. Be unapologetically YOU!

৪০৫৪

By choosing healthy over skinny you are choosing self-love over self-judgment. You are beautiful!

৪০৫৪

The Truth About Potentiality

We are beings of infinite potentiality. That sounds wonderful, but what does it mean to have infinite potential? If we are all so infinitely potential, why do very few of us experience happiness, good health, or success?

Remember this; the word "potential" is what the word "possible" becomes when it wears a tuxedo. It does not guarantee anything. It doesn't mean something WILL happen, it just means it CAN happen.

Potential remains an intangible possibility until you participate; until you ACT. You are the activator that bridges potentiality and reality. You are the point of origin for things to transcend from the realm of the possible to the tangible. Take action towards the life you desire!

When we do not take action, potentiality becomes the soil that houses the seeds of your regret.

We all know the regretful feeling of unrealized potential. We all know what it feels like to join a gym and not go... to feel a love we didn't express... to feel sorry but not apologize... to desire but not venture... to promise but not deliver... we have ALL been there.

I know you have heard the spiritual masters and gurus tell you how important your infinite potentiality is; that it could be the magical answer to your problems. But be aware of what their behavior says. When they sell you their products, do they ask you to promise you'll pay (potentiality) or do they require you to ACT and give them your credit card?

As authors of our own story of life, our potential is immeasurable. Don't let yourself rest on the magical idea that all things are possible; instead, make the choice to act upon the course of your goals and dreams.

This is a quantum universe that we experience as it is expressed through physical laws. Einstein said, "Nothing happens until something moves." What are you waiting for? Move! Your movement activates your potential.

> *There is no problem this universe can hand you that you aren't innately designed to solve. If it has been handed to you, it can be handled by you. This is the brilliant effectiveness of our design.*

ഇരു

Harness the power of today! Seize the blessings of today! Make something happen, enhance your life, make someone laugh, help a friend, love, love, love!

ഇരു

A very small percentage of the people in this world will actually experience and live today. So many people will be stuck on another day, another time that traumatized them and caused them to spiritually stutter so they miss out on this day.

ഇരു

Many people experience the travesty of regret in their end days; the realization that nothing held them back, that nothing was in their way, that there is no one to blame, only themselves. Don't just sit by waiting for your life to happen, make it happen! Don't just hope your dreams will come alive, breathe life into them! Don't let your fear help you birth a well-nourished regret. Take action today! At the end of the day, at the end of the year, at the end of your life, live in such a manner that you can hold your head up high, smile, and be proud of a life well lived.

ഇരു

Just because your pain is understandable, doesn't mean your behavior is acceptable.

ഇരു

ଛେଓଷ

Why would you give someone the power to tell you that you can't go further when they don't even know how far you've come?

ଛେଓଷ

At any given point you can release your greatest self. Don't let anyone hold you back. Don't let anyone dilute you. Don't be peer pressured into being less than you are. People willing to dilute themselves for the sake of others is one of the great tragedies of our time. Stop letting others define and set the pace for your life. Get out there and be your best. Do your best. Live your best. Make every day count and you'll see how exponentially more exciting, thrilling, successful, happy, and full your life will be.

ଛେଓଷ

It's called an '*accomplish*ment', not an '*intent*-ishment'. You've got to BE it to SEE it. NO MORE EXCUSES - Decide what you want, create a plan, and get your ass out there!

ଛେଓଷ

Sometimes there are stormy moments in your life when your friends do more than just walk with you; they become angels that carry you and protect you with their wings.

ଛେଓଷ

Notes to my Younger Self

Get rich quick schemes are for
the lazy and unambitious. Respect
your dreams enough to pay the
full price for them.

You're Not Rejected –
You're Redirected

We often have a diluted sense of self; we do not see the magnitude of the greatness inside of us. As a result, most people live within the parameters of the lowest part of their life; they dwell in the basement of their capability.

When you have a small picture of yourself, it distorts the size of the problems and challenges you face. You become easily intimidated and even more easily deterred from following your desired success. You look at mistakes as final and failures as unworthiness. You see a small YOU and a BIG everything else. The vision of yourself is distorted and the efficiency of your journey is burdened.

You are a reflection of greatness; don't lose sight of that! There have been countless challenges that you thought were bigger than you, but you're still here. They have not defeated you, they have not stopped you, and even if you didn't realize it, they had to bow to your innate superiority.

Keep your dream alive. Keep your relationship alive. Keep your career alive. Keep your goal alive. Live BIG! You have not been rejected, you have been redirected. Delayed, but not denied. You are greater than you can ever imagine! Let your journey be fueled and your body be nourished by your victorious past and move forward in the direction of your magnificent dreams. You are worthy; live accordingly.

This life is for loving, sharing, learning, smiling, caring, forgiving, laughing, hugging helping, dancing, wondering, healing, and even more loving. I choose to live life this way. I want to live my life in such a way that when I get out of bed in the morning, the devil says, "aw shit, he's up!"

৪৩

You can still make today the day you change yourself, love yourself, forgive yourself, respect yourself, honor yourself, cherish yourself, admire yourself, express yourself, be true to yourself... It's never too late!

৪৩

There is nothing better for your family than for you to be at your best, for you to be at your own peace, for you to be showing them in every way who you are, and what you stand for.

৪৩

Your life plays out as a reflection of your genetic makeup and potentiality as expressed through your environment and choices. Love yourself enough to create an environment in your life that is conducive to the nourishment of your personal growth. Allow yourself to let go of the people, thoughts, and situations that poison your well-being. Cultivate a vibrant surrounding and commit yourself to making choices that will help you release the greatest expression of your unique beauty and purpose.

৪৩

In many ways, life is about managing your delusions; keeping the ones that nourish and eliminating the ones that poison.

৪৩

৪০৫৪

You are a beautiful creation... perfectly imperfect... a work in progress... you have everything you need to fulfill your purpose... don't dilute yourself for any person or any reason... you are enough... be unapologetically you.

৪০৫৪

Tomorrow will never call to ask your opinion; you don't control it. Stop allowing today's possibilities to be robbed by tomorrow's insecurities.

৪০৫৪

We would do ourselves a tremendous favor by letting go of the people who poison our spirit.

৪০৫৪

Sometimes problems don't require a solution to solve them; instead they require maturity to outgrow them.

৪০৫৪

Act in gratitude today... If you are grateful to those you love, show them. If you are grateful to those who have helped you, show them. If you are grateful to your creator, to your family, to your friends, and you want it to be known, let it be shown!

৪০৫৪

The Essence of Beauty

There is nothing more rare, nor more beautiful, than a woman being unapologetically herself; comfortable in her perfect imperfection. To me, that is the true essence of beauty.

It seems that embracing your true self radiates a natural beauty that cannot be diluted or ignored. That beautiful, radiant essence is YOU. Confident, powerful, untamable, badass you!

Proudly embracing all of her perfect imperfections, a woman this empowered emanates the type of beauty that inspires poetry, songs, and powerful expressions of the heart's desires. A woman that powerful can exude a life-changing beauty, sensuality, and confidence; it's easy to see why the marketing industry spends gigantic amounts of money to convince you to NEVER feel this way.

If you know how beautiful you are, they can't sell you their products. That simple truth has been the source of the mass diluting of our beautiful women. Convinced they are not enough, convinced they are fatally flawed, convinced they are unworthy, and most importantly, convinced that they need your product to fix them.

Ladies, most of you have no idea how beautiful you are. Don't let an agenda-driven campaign designed to make you feel unattractive steal that beautiful radiant glow within. Do not become disconnected from the truth of your beauty.

You are beautiful by design... just the way you are.

৪৩

100% of a Guru's marketing plan depends on you holding the belief that you are not enough; that you were created less equipped than necessary to fulfill your purpose. What if you let go of that belief and connected with the truth of your innate power to change and shape your life? You ARE enough. You CAN change and shape your own life. Anyone who tells you different is simply lying. Your life has immeasurable potentiality for greatness; act accordingly.

৪৩

It has been noted that actions speak louder than words; in fact, I have found that during many situations in life, words are just noise and actions are the ONLY things that speak.

৪৩

Happiness, Success, Excellence: They are not something you get for knowing the path; they are something you experience by walking it.

৪৩

Your life is a reflection of how effectively you balance potential and kinetic energy.

৪৩

༺ঌ

There is nothing more rare, nor more beautiful, than a woman being unapologetically herself; comfortable in her perfect imperfection. To me, that is the true essence of beauty.

༺ঌ

Don't wait for other people to be loving, giving, compassionate, grateful, forgiving, generous, or friendly... lead the way!

༺ঌ

My past has not defined me, destroyed me, deterred me, or defeated me; it has only strengthened me.

༺ঌ

Embracing an attitude of gratitude is nourishing to the soul. When we allow ourselves to be engulfed in gratitude, this abundant soul nourishment overflows to your relationships, careers, and day to day lives.

༺ঌ

You are not a victim. No matter what you have been through, you're still here. You may have been challenged, hurt, betrayed, beaten, and discouraged, but nothing has defeated you. You are still here! You have been delayed but not denied. You are not a victim, you are a victor. You have a history of victory.

༺ঌ

Notes to my Younger Self

Pay attention to the behavior of
the most successful people.

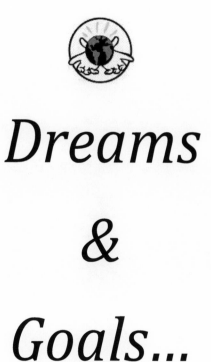

Dreams

&

Goals...

If Not Now, When?

If Not Now, When?

There are so many beautiful things happening right now.

Within all the beauty that radiates in this very moment, amongst all the happenings of the now, and woven within the fabric of this moment, you will find an abundance of opportunity.

This opportunity is available at all times and remains inactive and formless until YOU give it form and set it in motion.

How will you define and use the opportunity available to you?

Let today be the day you make the choice to no longer throw away the opportunities presented in each passing moment.

Seize the opportunity accessible in the NOW! Empower yourself to take hold of the opportunity for change, for decisions, for growth, for simplicity, for love, for forgiveness, for compassion, for happiness... the opportunity to live the life you've always wanted to live, to live in alignment with your dreams, to express your greatest self, to be unapologetically YOU... the opportunity to act on all of these things is present right now.

What are you willing to have left undone in your life?

We all have had so many goals, so many visions, and so many dreams for ourselves, yet we often put them on the back burner.

We put them on the back burner, not because we don't want to do it, but because we are convinced that a later time will be better. We are confident to the same degree that any gambler is confident.

Our confidence is rooted in the idea that we can pursue our goals, dreams, and desires at a later time and that it will somehow be an easier journey. But the reality is that the cemetery is full of books that were never written, full of chances that were never taken, full of relationships that were never started, full of resentments that were never mended... full of regret. The cemetery is full of gamblers that got it wrong.

Don't let yourself be another example of a life gambled but not lived. Do not waste another day!

If not now, when?

☙❧

Stop blaming outside circumstances for your inside chaos.

☙❧

One of the most healing things you can do is recognize where in your life you are your own poison.

☙❧

The beauty that radiates from someone freely expressing their uniqueness is enchanting.

☙❧

Once you understand how powerful you are within, you exponentially increase the power and potentiality of everything outside of you.

☙❧

There are times in my life when I have been medicine for some while poison for others. I used to think I was a victim of my story until I realized the truth, that I am the creator of my story. I choose what type of person I will be and what type of impact I will leave on others. I will never choose the destructive path of self and outward victimization again.

☙❧

Do you love yourself enough to BE what you love yourself enough to WANT?

☙❧

֎

We all make mistakes, have struggles, and even regret things in our past. But you are not your mistakes, you are not your struggles, and you are here NOW with the power to shape your day and your future.

֎

Some of the things I hated my parents for when I was younger are the same things I love my parents for now that I'm older.

֎

In your own life, it's important to know how spectacular you are.

֎

Like a gift, beautifully wrapped at the foot of your bed each morning, today asks that you open it and enjoy everything inside. Exhaust yourself with all it has to offer!

֎

Ladies, most of you have no idea how beautiful you are. Don't let mean words from an insecure soul blind you from the truth of your beauty. You are beautiful by design... just the way you are.

֎

Your opinion is not my reality.

֎

Know Where You Are Going

I'm often asked what the "secret" to my success is. My answer is that I don't have a secret; I have a method. I set a goal that I treat as a destination and I create a plan that I treat as a map. With my destination and map complete, I stay committed to the journey I have set.

There is no secret to success. There is a simple formula; journey in the direction of your dreams and goals and you will experience success. It is also no secret that along that journey there will be countless temptations to stray, detour, and stop. The challenge is in being committed enough to your vision to let nothing stand in your way.

Most people fall short. Not because they don't know a "secret" to success, but because they know what they want but haven't mapped out the way to get there and haven't accepted the price of commitment.

If you are ready for a change and if you are ready to start living the life you have always dreamed of, determine your destination and start moving. If you want to live the full beauty of your dream, be willing to pay the full price for it. The price for your dreams and success is paid each time you fight the temptation to get off course, each time you fight the desire to go back to the same old habits, and each time you keep going even though you want to quit.

Your dream life awaits; be willing to love yourself enough to pay the price for it.

Get out of your own way... stop the paralysis by analysis... dream your dream... then, WAKE UP and bring it to life!

೫൪ഌ

Today is a new day. It's a day you have never seen before and will never see again. Stop telling yourself the "same crap, different day" lie! How many days has that lie stolen from you? Seize the wonder and uniqueness of today! Recognize that throughout this beautiful day, you have an incredible amount of opportunities to move your life in the direction you want it to go.

೫൪ഌ

Resolutions are most often empty promises for those who have an abundance of dreams, but refuse to wake up and live them.

೫൪ഌ

When we see someone or something as imperfect, it is a reflection of our limitations, not theirs.

೫൪ഌ

You were born to journey in the direction of your purpose. Anything that halts your progress is contrary to your design.

೫൪ഌ

If you can transcend from the dark rut of disempowered thinking to the bright light of an empowered agreement with reality, you will see opportunities not barriers. You will see the finish line, not the hurdles.

೫൪ഌ

൫ൠ

Don't give up! It's not over. The universe is balanced. Every set-back bears with it the seeds of a come-back.

൫ൠ

I promise you nothing is as chaotic as it seems. Nothing is worth your health. Nothing is worth poisoning yourself into stress, anxiety, and fear.

൫ൠ

As I look back on my life, I realize that every time I thought I was being rejected from something good, I was actually being re-directed to something better.

൫ൠ

The problem that we have with a victim mentality is that we forget to see the blessings of the day. Because of this, our spirit is poisoned instead of nourished.

൫ൠ

A life of happiness, peace, and love is all within our grasp. We are always just one choice away.

൫ൠ

I find that I am most happy and healthy when I am living in alignment with my goals, dreams, and principles.

൫ൠ

Notes to my Younger Self

Write down five character traits you admire most in your personal heroes. You now have a list of traits to emulate in your own life.

Little Steps

Ambitious goals can sometimes be overwhelming. Here is a tip to get past the sometimes staggering visualization of monumental change:

Set small achievable goals each day. It ensures little victories throughout the day and keeps you motivated and on target for your greater goals. Don't forget that success isn't a destination; it's the experience of a purposeful journey. So by setting small frequent goals, you fuel the long journey with a nourishing feeling of success.

Move with purpose in the direction of the change you seek in your life. Take little steps, stay on course, and enjoy the experience of success.

> *You're better than the life you've settled for. RISE to the challenge of your dreams! Don't just dream it – LIVE it!*

ಶೂಧ

You were not meant for a mundane or mediocre life!

ಶೂಧ

At every given moment we are absolutely perfect for what is required for our journey.

ಶೂಧ

Life is a balanced system of learning and evolution. Whether pleasure or pain; every situation in your life serves a purpose. It is up to us to recognize what that purpose could be.

ಶೂಧ

I will be generous with my love today. I will sprinkle compliments and uplifting words everywhere I go. I will do this knowing that my words are like seeds and when they fall on fertile soil, a reflection of those seeds will grow into something greater.

ಶೂಧ

You are here with a unique purpose. Stop letting others define you. Stop letting others dilute you. Don't be bullied or pressured into being less than you are.

ಶೂಧ

The empowered woman is powerful beyond measure and beautiful beyond description.

ಶೂಧ

৪০৫৪

Love and compassion are the mother and father of a smile. We need to create more smiles in our world today. Smiles, after all, pave the way to a happy world.

৪০৫৪

Holding a grudge and harboring anger/resentment is poison to the soul. Get even with people... but not those who have hurt us; forget them, instead get even with those who have helped us.

৪০৫৪

The way you live each day is a sentence in the story of your life. Every day, you make the choice whether the sentence ends with a period, question mark, or exclamation point.

৪০৫৪

There is nothing worse for the lying soul than the mirror of reality.

৪০৫৪

We must remember balance and moderation. Patience can be spiritually enriching and virtuous... but when taken in excess, it turns into procrastination; the poison of inaction.

৪০৫৪

When Things Get Cold

When serving in the United States Air Force, I got to see some beautiful places and experience a myriad of different people and climates. One of these climates was right here in the U.S.A.; North Dakota.

Although scenically beautiful and home to some of the nicest people I've met, it was very cold and windy. The extreme cold weather prompted for winter survival training. During the training we learned that the reason your fingers and toes are the first to feel the damaging effects of the cold is because they are extremities that are furthest from your warm-blood pumping heart. To fight off the damaging effects, wiggle them. The movements get the blood flowing again.

Over the years, I have learned that the same principle can be applied to our everyday lives. If your career, relationships, business, dreams, or goals are "cold," it is because they are furthest from your heart. Take some time to clear out the nonsense that has gained your heart's attention and re-focus on what matters.

Keep your goals, hopes, and dreams close to your heart by acting on them daily. Let actions that are aligned with your intent get the warm blood of life-potentiality flowing to your relationship, career, ambitions, and dreams. When things in your life get cold; MOVE!

৪৩

Most haters are stuck in a poisonous mental prison of jealousy and self-doubt that blinds them to their own potentiality.

৪৩

I don't have time, energy, or interest in hating the haters; I'm too busy loving the lovers.

৪৩

Don't throw away another day! No more procrastinating! Only YOU can make it happen. So, UN-ASS the couch and make it happen!

৪৩

Pay attention to what you pray for. Your prayers are not just a reflection of your desires and hopes; they are a guide for personal behavior. Pray it, BE it, and you will SEE it.

৪৩

Being a hater is a measurement of cowardice.

৪৩

We are designed with a dreaming brain and a hopeful spirit; it is our nature to envision the life of our dreams. And while dreaming comes easy to us, we must never forget that it takes strength, dedication, and courageous action to bring that dream to life.

৪৩

୫୦ର

Just like your body and lifestyle can be healthy or unhealthy, the same is true with your beliefs. Your beliefs can be your medicine or your poison.

୫୦ର

New levels bring new devils. Stay unapologetically committed to your goals and let go of anyone who poisons your spirit.

୫୦ର

It is our action that determines the viability of our dream.

୫୦ର

Stop trying to "fix" yourself; you're NOT broken! You are perfectly imperfect and powerful beyond measure.

୫୦ର

Each day gives the opportunity for you to be treated right, to feel worthy, and to be successful. It's a choice you have to make, faith you have to embrace, and a standard you have to set.

୫୦ର

You are the point of origin for everything in your world: you set the standard for yourself.

୫୦ର

Notes to my Younger Self

Statistics lie. They are designed to sway opinions. Take the time to keep yourself informed on things that matter.

Your Defining Moment

You would not be here today if yesterday was your defining moment. Don't let life trick you into the impossible task of fixing a day that has already passed. Think of how much time has been lost and how much energy has been wasted in this unfruitful way of living.

Yesterday was not your defining moment. The calendar moved forward; why not you?

This new day offers you the sustenance you need to proceed on your life's expedition. Yesterday's sustenance has spoiled; the nutrition of yesterday has become the poison of today. Let it go.

Be fueled by the opportunities of today. Do not be passive in your life. Be courageous in driving forward in this journey of life. I know people will try to push you back. I know life will challenge you to find refuge in the past. I know the present induces fear. Do not be fooled into backwards living. Be courageous enough to keep moving forward.

Let yesterday be what it is; a reference point. It is not a reflection of where you're going, it's a reflection of where you were. Drive forward! Think of your car, its purpose, and how it's designed. The purpose of your car is to help you effectively navigate your journey. Its design is one with a large windshield that faces forward and a small mirror that faces behind. When you drive, you are very attentive to what is in front of you and you use the rear-view mirror as a quick reference to aid any adjustments to your journey.

We are having a human experience; a life that moves forward whether we like it or not. Choose to stop hindering the effectiveness of your own journey by driving with the rear-view mirror. The life behind you is a reference point; use it wisely as such. As for today, look ahead and drive towards your dreams!

The magic that turns dreams into reality is YOU! When you are inspired by a dream, create a good plan; that turns it into a goal. Then, live your life in a way that will bring that dream, that goal, to life. The magic is you.

80C8

Become the leader of your life. Lead yourself to where you want to be. Breathe life back into your ambitions, your desires, your goals, your relationships.

80C8

Free yourself from the need to blame others. There are two reasons that you are where you are right now; action or inaction.

80C8

Intent without dedicated action is simply not enough. Action without a clear intent is a waste. It is when these two powerful forces are aligned that the energy of the universe conspires in your favor.

80C8

The word "seek" is a verb. Are you treating it as such in your life? If you seek change, success, or love; DO it - BE it!

80C8

Luck is a word the bitter teach to the ignorant.

80C8

Today's man should do more than just talk; he should act. He should do more than just promise; he should deliver.

80C8

৪০৫৪

Fear has the role we give it. We are able to empower or poison ourselves to whatever degree we want. This is the beauty of our design.

৪০৫৪

You are beautiful. Know this. Anyone who tells you otherwise is simply lying. You are beautiful.

৪০৫৪

You have had a dream for so many years. Let today be the day you make a plan for it. Just think about how much more likely you are to hit your target when you finally aim at it.

৪০৫৪

If you have a goal, write it down. If you do not write it down, you do not have a goal - you have a wish.

৪০৫৪

Happiness, success, peace, and love are experienced when we live accordingly. They are not something you have, they are something you DO.

৪০৫৪

Don't nourish your fears more than you nourish your hopes.

৪০৫৪

Action is the universal language of success.

৪০৫৪

The Difference Between
Bravery & Courage

I learned many priceless lessons during my time serving in the military. And while many of those lessons were delivered through serious situations, there are some that were delivered with humor. The lesson in the difference between bravery and courage is one of them.

I had been nominated for a leadership award and even though I was honored to be considered, I couldn't help but ask the Master Sergeant why I was selected over the many brave soldiers they had to choose from.

He said, "You're right, all of these soldiers are brave men and women; but you... you are courageous. That is why you have been selected." I think he saw the look of bewilderment on my young face. He continued, "Maraboli, there is a difference between bravery and courage. I'm going to tell you the difference and I want you to always remember this... any BRAVE man will grab a lion by its balls, but it takes COURAGE to keep squeezing."

I have never forgotten that lesson because sometimes in life, we've got to keep squeezing. It may have taken bravery for you to get moving, to go back to school, to get back into your relationship, for you to trust again, to love again, to want to go back into the career field, to start your business, to act on your dreams; but sometimes, bravery is not enough. Sometimes, once you're in the thick of it, you've got to keep squeezing... keep squeezing and not give up.

If life knocks you down, you've got to get up. It's not about not having problems. The only people who don't have problems are the people who aren't living anymore. Happiness is not the absence of problems; it's the ability to deal with them. Don't be disillusioned into thinking that you'll eventually get to a point where you are so enlightened, so intelligent, so spiritual, and so scientific, you've got it so figured out that you won't have any problems. Save yourself the energy and attachment to the nonsense of that idea. Life will always deliver you challenges; how you respond will determine the reward you reap. Keep squeezing!

> With no action to nourish it, your dream becomes a fantasy.

೫೦೦೩

A sense of entitlement is a cancerous thought process that is void of gratitude and can be deadly to relationships, businesses, and even nations.

೫೦೦೩

Success isn't something you have, it's something you do. Don't be fooled into taking shortcuts, they always lead to a dead-end. Instead, establish a goal, make a plan, and take purposeful action. Those who experience success are those who live it; those who earn it.

೫೦೦೩

Cemeteries are full of unfulfilled dreams... countless echoes of "could have" and "should have"... countless books unwritten... countless songs unsung... I want to live my life in such a way that when my body is laid to rest, it will be a well needed rest from a life well lived, a song well sung, a book well written, opportunities well explored, and a love well expressed.

೫೦೦೩

Participate in your dreams today. There are unlimited opportunities available with this new day. Take action on those wonderful dreams you've had in your mind for so long. Remember, success is something you experience when you act accordingly.

೫೦೦೩

Every step towards your dream today is a step away from your regret tomorrow.

೫೦೦೩

ဆာ

You were not meant for a life of mediocrity! Stop letting the regret of yesterday and the insecurity of tomorrow steal your today. Live this day! Do not allow your spirit to be softened or your happiness to be limited by a day you cannot have back or a day that does not yet exist. Take charge! Seize this day and allow upon this fertile day to be planted the seeds of your happiness and success.

ဆာ

I find that being considerate of others and keeping what I say and what I do in agreement makes for a great night's sleep.

ဆာ

Celebrate your victories! Be verbal about it. Haters will say you're bragging, but those who love you will celebrate with you.

ဆာ

ACT on your dreams! It is not enough to just want it. Don't throw away another day. Take action and watch them come alive!

ဆာ

When you're crying, your tears may be watering the seeds of your come-back.

ဆာ

Notes to my Younger Self

Be the type of man a wife would cherish and a child would admire.

The People on Your Board

Sometimes we don't realize that we allow certain people access and influence in areas of our lives that they aren't actually qualified for. As we escalate our success and expand the depth of our personal and professional potentiality, it becomes vital to examine the people we allow into our inner-circle of influence.

Look at the corporate model: Corporations have a board that consists of individuals who specialize in different fields and lend their expertise accordingly. The purpose of this board system is to ensure that a business can maximize its potentiality in each field of its endeavors.

I understand that I am not a corporation, but I have built and successfully run several of them. I find this model of compartmentalized expertise to be highly efficient and effective. When we need marketing, we have a team for that. When we need accounting, we have a team for that. When we need graphic design, we have a team for that... you get the point. I wouldn't ask the accountant for advice on graphic design. This "board" system, when run correctly, has helped many businesses and organizations maximize their potential.

In my personal life I am blessed to have many friends. This being true, I still tend to keep a "board" of friends that I refer to for their expertise for different parts of my life. I refer to my successful friends when I want to know about business, my healthy friends when I'm curious about health, etc...

I find that when I didn't have this system, like most people, I would tend to take ALL of my advice from a certain friend, even though they weren't qualified to have such influence. Taking relationship advice from someone who isn't in one, or money advice from someone who has none, or health advice from someone who is overweight, doesn't make for good results.

Friendship is a beautiful blessing. You may love your friends and they may love you, but that doesn't mean they should have unexamined influence in all areas of your life. Pay attention to who you have on your life's "board" and make the adjustments necessary to ensure both your friendships and your goals remain healthy and intact.

> Pay attention! At all moments of the day you are either leading or being led.

ৰাওে

Rename your "To-Do" list to your "Opportunities" list. Each day is a treasure chest filled with limitless opportunities; take joy in checking many off your list.

ৰাওে

I am not a victim. No matter what I have been through, I'm still here. I have a history of victory.

ৰাওে

The world gives us PLENTY of opportunities to strengthen our patience. While this truth can definitely be challenging, this is a good thing. Patience is a key that unlocks the door to a more fulfilling life. It is through a cultivation of patience that we become better parents, powerful teachers, great businessmen, good friends, and live a happier life.

ৰাওে

What we instill in our children will be the foundation upon which they build their future.

ৰাওে

The journey of success requires a map for effective navigation. Establish a destination by defining what you want. Once you have a destination, take physical action by making choices that move you towards that destination.

ৰাওে

ॐ

Your dream is a visualized reflection of your potential and only YOU have the ability to bring it to life.... you are more than just the dreamer, you are the point of origin for its reality.

ॐ

The victim mindset produces a delusion of fault and blame that blinds you from the simple truth of cause and effect.

ॐ

Most board meetings amount to little more than intellectual masturbation. There are ideas that cause thrills, chills, and satisfaction, but there is no impregnation. Nothing is ever born of them. It's intellectual masturbation.

ॐ

This is your life. This is your moment. Think of all you have been through just to get here... MAKE IT COUNT!

ॐ

Be mindful of your social environment. By nature, the group you hang-out with will develop a common behavior and mindset. This behavior usually gravitates towards the lowest common denominator. Choose your group wisely.

ॐ

Paralysis by Analysis

It's easy to get caught up in deep analysis of our plans to change our lives. It's also easy to not realize how we are often paralyzed by the over-analysis, and how much time this action-stalling thought process steals from us.

Avoid paralysis by analysis. Don't get too caught up in the analysis of your plan. Just have a specific intent, a specific destination, and start moving. Adjustments can be made along the way. Making changes in your life is like driving a stick-shift car; the hardest part is to get the initial gear and begin motion. After that, life is more forgiving for adjustments. So, determine the direction and get moving!

●　●　●

The only permission, the only
validation, and the only
opinion that matters in our
quest for greatness is our own.

●　●　●

৪৩

Have a clear goal and plan. Waste no effort in your journey. Be strong, committed, and effective and you will experience a level of success few will ever know.

৪৩

Smile at strangers and you just might change a life.

৪৩

The people we consider successful in our society are all people that seize every moment and make the best of each situation.

৪৩

It doesn't matter if you're 20, 40, 60, 80, or 100. Embrace your sexy-ass self and express it!

৪৩

If at first you don't succeed, you're doing it wrong. Learn from the experience. Try again, but with a different approach.

৪৩

You've been given the innate power to shape your life.

৪৩

Great changes in our society are always inspired and set in motion by one person. Be that person today.

৪৩

ಬೂ ೧೩

What do you think will be more effective when it comes to succeeding, believing you can or KNOWING you will? Let today be the last day you took timid steps of belief, and start taking confident steps of purpose-driven knowing!

ಬೂ ೧೩

It's funny how, in this journey of life, even though we may begin at different times and places, our paths cross with others so that we may share our love, compassion, observations, and hope. This is a design of God that I appreciate and cherish.

ಬೂ ೧೩

Today I will take the opportunity to do unanticipated good.

ಬೂ ೧೩

Stop being a victim of your days and start being the creator and shaper of those same days.

ಬೂ ೧೩

Life is a miracle. YOU are a unique expression of this purposeful miracle. Think of how GREAT that makes you. Live big! You are not here to dwell within the basement of your potentiality.

ಬೂ ೧೩

Notes to my Younger Self

Don't lie. Life is a puzzle and we are all unique pieces. When you lie, you make it impossible to find your true place in the grand design.

Get the Peanut Butter

Millions upon millions of books have been sold in the marketing frenzy that fooled people into believing there was a secret way of "thinking" yourself into success. Millions of books sold, but how many of those people actually attracted and realized their new fortunes by simply "intending?"

While it can be spiritually and emotionally intoxicating to think so, free-yourself from the ineffective belief that your intent alone can create material results. Embrace your spirituality, but don't turn your back on your humanity. Apply reason and rationality to the ideas marketing companies try to sell you. Remember, they are targeting you for an emotional response. Emotional responses get you to buy their products. Think before you act. The material world works around material laws; not mystical ones.

For example, let's say you're making a peanut butter and jelly sandwich. You have the bread, the jelly, and when you go to the cupboard to get the peanut butter, you find that you have none. What will get you peanut butter? Will prayer alone do it? Will meditation alone do it? Will putting together a vision board do it? Will repeating affirmations do it? Of course not! While all of those things are fantastic for spiritual and emotional health, the ONLY thing that will get peanut butter into your cupboard and on your sandwich is your action!

Even though magical thinking can be intoxicating and inspire amazing dreams, don't forget that it is in finding a balance between your spirituality and your humanity, the subjective and the objective, that you will generate the results you desire. It is when you have an intent (in this case, the need for peanut butter) and you align it with your actions (actually going to get it) that you will have success in the material world.

> *Stop allowing your outdated ideas to hinder your progress. Become open to new information that can refine, improve, and enhance your way of thinking. This will empower your way of living.*

෫ඖ

It's time for a spring cleaning of your thoughts, it's time to stop to just existing it's time to start living.

෫ඖ

A goal that is not planned is a wish; a dream that is not chased is a fantasy.

෫ඖ

You did not go through everything you've gone through just to end up in the same place you were when you started. Let your past be your spring-board, not your quicksand.

෫ඖ

If the future you see for yourself is greatly different than your life now, the actions that you take must also be greatly different. You cannot do the same thing and get something different.

෫ඖ

Although goals are important, having a plan of action is vital to the success of those goals. Having a goal with no plan of action is like wanting to travel to a new destination without having a map.

෫ඖ

Never compromise your values.

෫ඖ

കര

We must never forget that while striving to leave a better planet to our kids, it is just as important that we strive to leave better kids to our planet.

കര

A lot of the conflict you have in your life exists simply because you're not living in alignment; you're not being true to yourself.

കര

You cannot continue on the same path and arrive at a different destination. Make the choice to have your actions reflect your goals.

കര

When we're not true to our thoughts and not true to the feelings we have deep inside, we find ourselves unhappy. Be courageous enough to align your life with your feelings, desires, and sense of purpose.

കര

Plant seeds of happiness, hope, success, and love; it will all come back to you in abundance. This is the law of nature.

കര

INTENT reveals desire; ACTION reveals commitment.

കര

Take One Step and Repeat

It is easy to be discouraged at the mountain of change we seek in our lives. At the same time, it's important to remember that the mountain of change, just like an actual mountain, can only be scaled one step at a time.

I'm reminded of an encounter I had with an old-friend from school. I ran into him at the local bank and we began to catch-up. He told me about his health issues and that his doctor told him he needed to lose 50 pounds. Needless to say, he was stressed out about the monumental level of this weight-loss challenge. He felt discouraged and confessed to me that he didn't even know where to begin to change his life in a way to drop 50 pounds.

I told him, "You don't need to figure out how to lose 50 pounds. You just need to make the adjustment in your life to lose 1 pound. Adjust your diet, learn to mentally cope with cravings, and begin to incorporate exercise into your routine. Do what you need to do in order to create a lifestyle system in which you can lose 1 pound... and follow THAT system 50 times."

To date, he lost the weight he needed to lose and then some; while at the same time, he gained understanding and emotional strength to apply the same systems to other endeavors in his life.

One step at a time...

೩೦೧೩

You unlock the door to greater levels of excellence and success when you accept who you are. It is from this point of acceptance that we can create a masterful life.

೩೦೧೩

Success is not about your techniques, it's not solely about the wisdom or the knowledge you have, it's about your mindset and your actions.

೩೦೧೩

No more excuses or procrastination! Stop allowing your days to be stolen by busy nothingness and take calculated steps towards your goals.

೩೦೧೩

Pretend those around you are deaf to your words. Let your actions speak and communicate your feelings and intentions. This way of living ensures the potency of your message is delivered and serves as a gauge against our verbal nonsense.

೩೦೧೩

I don't know when my time on earth will be up; but I DO know that today, I am one day closer. You can bet I'm going to make this day count! Will you?

೩೦೧೩

୫୦୧

Stop focusing on what you don't want; it's a tremendous waste of time and energy. Instead, start focusing on what you do want. This is the only way to create a plan of action which will enable you to experience the life you envision.

୫୦୧

There are often great lessons to be learned at the roots of stress, drama, and heartache. Don't let the magnitude of the circumstance blind you to the value of the lesson.

୫୦୧

Do what you think is right. Don't let people make the decision of right or wrong for you.

୫୦୧

The only way you can own this moment is to evict the victim mentality from the dwelling of your mind.

୫୦୧

Sometimes people are disempowered because they subconsciously identify themselves by their temporary circumstances instead of connecting with their innate value and truth.

୫୦୧

Notes to my Younger Self

Be more than a father, be a dad.

Be more than a figure,

be an example.

Life

&

Happiness...

Each Day is a Lifetime

The idea of each new day being a birth to new opportunities and a clean slate is not a new one. We often hear about the importance of seeing a new day as a fresh start; and while talking about the birth of a new day is insightful for a happy and successful life, I feel a very important piece is left out; recognizing its death.

Each day presents you with a lifetime of living. There are ups and downs, wins and losses, chances to love, to forgive, to dare, to hope, to move towards your goals and dreams, to change for the better... each day is a clean slate and each day is a lifetime.

The burden of the past...

Accumulating the weight of your yesterdays is a common source of stress. There have been countless books, movies, and sermons on the importance of letting go. I think one of the reasons we have trouble letting go is that we aren't ever conditioned to do so; we get conditioned to moving on to the new and exciting, but we aren't reminded to let go of the last thing. So we end up birthing many new days, many new situations, many new relationships, etc... but we never give a proper send-off to the ones that have passed.

A funeral for your day...

Rise to the incredible potential of each new day and exhaust yourself with all it has to offer. Take in all the things that can help you experience your greatest self and let the rest go. At the end of your day, have a funeral; think about the good and the bad of the day. Take the lessons and leave the drama. It's all about closure. It only takes a few minutes but makes an incredible difference.

This process helps you wake up to a new day without the heavy burden of all your yesterdays. How would your life be different if you had a funeral for each day? What about a funeral for past relationships or situations that still weigh heavily on you? Think of how liberating it would feel to have a funeral for past drama. Take the time to look back and give the past its proper recognition. Recognize it for its impact on your life and most importantly, recognize it for what it is... gone! Let go!

Each day is a lifetime. Live it to the max. Be unapologetically enthusiastic in your drive towards your dreams and goals. Let each day be lived in such a way that you find yourself hitting the pillow each night with a peaceful sense of satisfaction that can only come from a day well lived. Then, have a funeral for your day... let go and do the same tomorrow.

୫୦ଓଃ

When I accept myself, I am freed from the burden of needing you to accept me.

୫୦ଓଃ

It takes BRAVERY to recognize where in your life you are your own poison... it takes COURAGE to do something about it.

୫୦ଓଃ

If you want change and don't make choices that reflect the change, you are making a choice to keep things the same.

୫୦ଓଃ

If you want to find happiness, find gratitude.

୫୦ଓଃ

One of life's challenging realizations is that sometimes you outgrow your friends.

୫୦ଓଃ

It's simple; be YOU. If you're not being you, you're being someone else. YOU are not here to be someone else.

୫୦ଓଃ

The only thing that makes life unfair is the delusion that it should be fair.

୫୦ଓଃ

ೞେ

Happiness is a state of mind, a choice, a way of living; it is not something to be achieved, it is something to be experienced.

ೞେ

I am so grateful for my troubles. As I reflect back on my life, I have come to realize that my greatest triumphs have been born of my greatest troubles.

ೞେ

There is a difference between talented people and gifted people. Talented people are good AT something; Gifted people ARE that something.

ೞେ

We're a society that creates super heroes who aren't really super heroes. They are just regular people who live in alignment with their goals and dreams. They don't just talk about it, the LIVE it. You can choose to do the same.

ೞେ

Over-analysis is a dream killer. Sometimes you can drown yourself in your own thoughts.

ೞେ

Let today be the day you learn the grace of letting go and the power of moving on.

ೞେ

Life's Ingredients

How would your life be different if you learned to let go of things that have already let go of you? Your life is a blend of the ingredients you add to it. Whether you feel energetic or drained, nourished or poisoned, free or burdened, enthusiastic or indifferent; your subjective experience of life is a result of the ingredients you allow to stew in your mind and body.

From relationships long gone, to old grudges, to regrets, to all the "could've" and "should've," to the dead friendships you still hang on to, to all the broken resolutions; these are all expired life-moments that continue to be factors in the experience of your current life.

Let today be the day you consciously take inventory of the ingredients you ingest in your life's stew. Empower yourself to get rid of the elements that have long spoiled and no longer nourish. You wouldn't drink spoiled milk. You wouldn't eat rotten food. You wouldn't butter moldy bread. We all know that if you did any of these things, you would feel ill.

So, just as you wouldn't allow yourself to take in expired things for your meal; don't allow yourself to take in expired things for your life. Could that be the reason you feel spiritually or emotionally ill?

Do not let yesterday's events spoil today's moments. There is so much goodness around you. So many things that can nourish your mind, body, and soul. Allow yourself the nourishing fuel that today has to offer. Nourish your life with empowering ingredients. Make peace with the hurtful past. Stop letting it be part of the recipe for your daily life and let the past be what it is; an expired moment in time.

Let today be the day you are no longer intimidated by the monumental size of the change you want, but instead be empowered by your ability to make that change one step at a time.

ഇന്‍

We each contribute our own book to the great library of humanity.

ഇന്‍

Stop pointing fingers and placing blame on others. Your life can only change to the degree that you accept responsibility for it.

ഇന്‍

Some of the most powerful speeches I have given have been delivered in the dedicated silence of my actions.

ഇന്‍

If you are not the hero of your own story, then you're missing the whole point of your humanity.

ഇന്‍

Letting go means to come to the realization that some people are a part of your history, but not a part of your destiny.

ഇന്‍

The quest of discovering your empowered self is a process of refinement, not accumulation. Cut away the nonsense, the drama, the regret, the scars of the past, and make a decision to no longer let them govern your happiness and freedom.

ഇന്‍

80CR

The truth is, unless you let go, unless you forgive yourself, unless you forgive the situation, unless you realize that that situation is over, you cannot move forward.

80CR

Life is too short to waste time waiting for other people's approval on how you live it.

80CR

From warm meals, to daily exercise, to healthcare; one can't help but wonder how our society would be different if we tended to the elderly as we do to our imprisoned.

80CR

Your life isn't behind you; your memories are behind you. Your life is ALWAYS ahead of you. Today is a new day - seize it!

80CR

A lot of books in the self-help section of your bookstore really belong in the fiction section.

80CR

Cry. Forgive. Learn. Move on. Let your tears water the seeds of your future happiness.

80CR

Notes to my Younger Self

When you make a mistake, give an apology without an excuse attached to it. The longer an apology, the less authentic it is.

Car Manufacturer

Years ago, I was invited to a car manufacturing and testing facility. This was a facility at which engineers designed and tested several different types of automobiles. Each design was placed through a series of tests, including the wind tunnel.

While I don't know much about the design or manufacturing of cars, the wind tunnel test was very interesting to watch. A deep-white smoke blows through the tunnel and around the cars as the engineers gauge the resistance and calculate the aerodynamic values.

As I was watching them conduct this test, I asked one of the engineers, "What's the purpose of what you're doing here?" The engineer answered, "We put the car through this process so we can maximize its efficiency and effectiveness." I further inquired, "So after you conduct these tests, do you make adjustments to the engine as you feel necessary?" The engineer answered, "No, there isn't any need to do that; the engine it comes with is fine. It's the stuff that we add-on afterwards that causes drag. The things we attach to the original design sometimes cause the car to decline in its effectiveness and efficiency."

After hearing his response I couldn't help but see the correlation between this process and our own journey through this human experience. We are created masterfully; the engine we come with is fine. It's the stuff we pick up along the journey that slows us down. It's the stuff that we pick up along the journey that affects us adversely – it affects our efficiency, our speed, and our ability to navigate through this journey of life. It's the drama, regret, grudges, emotional scars, and other stuff we pick up along the way that hinders our progress.

Think of how much more efficiently and effectively you could drive towards your dreams if you cut away the stuff that causes drag... Let today be the day you free yourself from the drama, the issues, the self-destructive patterns, the poisonous people... drop the stuff that causes drag and happily move towards the life you want.

> *The volume of your voice does not increase the validity of your argument.*

ഔൗ

Don't let other people's opinions distort your reality. Be true to yourself. Be bold in pursuing your dreams. Be unapologetically you!

ഔൗ

It's not just about what I can SEE for our future, or humanity; it's about what I can DO for our future and humanity.

ഔൗ

The road to success is always under construction.

ഔൗ

You must learn to let go. Release the stress. You were never in control anyway.

ഔൗ

Life doesn't get easier or more forgiving; we get stronger and more resilient.

ഔൗ

An empowered life begins with serious personal questions about one's self. Those answers bear the seeds of success.

ഔൗ

Never run from the truth. It is always there; it never changes – save your energy.

ഔൗ

80CR

How would your life be different if instead of spending your energy and focus on hating those who hate you, you spent your energy and focus on loving those who love you?

80CR

Empowerment is being aware that there is no one to blame for my choices and actions; that I have a personal choice and responsibility for my life.

80CR

Beware: It is a quick transition from a nourishing sense of gratitude to a poisonous sense of entitlement.

80CR

I find few things more personally enriching than exploring the parameters of my own ignorance.

80CR

Challenges in life can either enrich you or poison you. You are the one who decides.

80CR

It's such an amazing awakening to realize that nothing in this universe happens TO YOU, 100% happens FOR YOU.

80CR

You're Not Drowning

You are not broken. You are not ugly. You are not unworthy. You are not too short. You are not too tall. You are not the number on a scale. You are not too old. You are not too young. You are not your mistakes.

You are a person designed with a purpose and the greatness within to bring that purpose to life. Whether it's cosmetic companies, latest diet fads, self-help or spiritual gurus, or numerous other agencies, this is a truth the marketing world NEVER wants you to know. They can't sell you a life-vest unless they can convince you that you're drowning. So they spend enormous amounts of money creating an advertising blitz that is 100% designed to have you feel broken enough to need their products.

You're not drowning. You are a unique gift to this world. Don't let psychological warfare from an advertisement campaign blind you from the truth of your beauty, possibility, worthiness, and purpose. Stop chasing what you already have. Your greatest self is never caused by a product; it is revealed by a choice to embrace your truth. Anyone who tells you differently is trying to convince you you're less than what you are; that you're broken... so they can sell you the fix.

ഇൻൽ

Our moral economy went bankrupt long before our financial one.

ഇൻൽ

Don't look for society to give you permission to be yourself.

ഇൻൽ

I will never let someone else's opinion define my reality.

ഇൻൽ

Although initially only few in numbers, it seems my gray hairs have launched an effective peer-pressure campaign intended to convert the others.

ഇൻൽ

You can't fly if your wings are holding the baggage of yesterday. Let go. Fly.

ഇൻൽ

Never again will I underestimate the greatness inside of me just because of the hate and limited thinking inside of others.

ഇൻൽ

A mindset of gratitude lifts the veil of bitterness and allows you to see beauty and possibility.

ഇൻൽ

୫୦୯ଃ

It is amazing how your life changes when you embrace the reality that you're better than the life you've settled for.

୫୦୯ଃ

We have an internal check and balance system. By design we are so filled with possibility, with opportunity, with greatness, that when we live small, within the bottom of our capability, we innately know we should be living greater than that, and it creates a disconnect inside that leads us to feeling empty, unhappy, and maybe even depressed.

୫୦୯ଃ

I have come to believe that our innate purpose is nothing more than to be the greatest version of ourselves. It is a process of refinement, improvement, and enhancement. When you are aligned with this process and living your purpose, you have the potential of creating something amazing.

୫୦୯ଃ

Love yourself. Forgive yourself. Be true to yourself. How you treat yourself sets the standard for how others will treat you.

୫୦୯ଃ

Country music is the poetry of the American spirit.

୫୦୯ଃ

Notes to my Younger Self

Pray. Not just with your words,
but with your actions.

Keep Your Eyes on Your Own Plate

"Keep your eyes on your own plate and enjoy your meal!" This was my mom's repetitive mantra at the dinner table in the late 70's as she surely fought off the urge to dropkick my brother and I while we argued about who got more mashed potatoes, or too many vegetables, or not the same amount of rice, etc...

At the time, I don't think she was trying to convey wisdom as much as she was simply trying to get us to shut-up, but still, there is DEEP wisdom in this mantra. How would your life be different if you kept your eyes on your own plate and enjoyed your meal?

We seem to go through life chasing the intangible. We even have an expression, "keeping up with the Jones'," that we use to describe this chase. At some point in our lives, usually when it's too late, we realize the Jones' are full of shit... they are in debt too, they have marital problems too, they have issues with their kids too, they stress about their career too... while you were trying to keep up with them, they were trying to keep up with you. Now you're both in it deep.

Keep your eyes on your own plate and enjoy your meal. This doesn't mean you shouldn't endeavor for more; I think it's our human nature to move towards growth and success. But when doing so, don't let the quest for more blind you to what you already have. Give yourself the time to be grateful for what you already have. Let the gratitude for today fuel you on your journey towards tomorrow. There is no greater way to dilute your own blessings than to compare them with, what you perceive, is the blessings of another. Enjoy what you have. Be grateful. Move in the direction of your own personal growth and success; not that of another. Be you; you will NEVER be great at being someone else.

> *There is emotional and psychological nourishment to be found in adopting a mindset of gratitude. A grateful mindset can set you free from the prison of disempowerment and the shackles of misery.*

&ᴏ&

Just because we're related, doesn't mean we're family.

&ᴏ&

Sometimes it seems that those with the greatest disregard for our laws are the same people in charge of creating or enforcing them.

&ᴏ&

Spread your happiness to others and let them spread theirs to you.

&ᴏ&

Stop giving your life away to other people.

&ᴏ&

The more I understand the mind and the human experience, the more I begin to suspect there is no such thing as unhappiness; there is only ungratefulness.

&ᴏ&

The reason many people in our society are miserable, sick, and highly stressed is because of an unhealthy attachment to things they have no control over.

&ᴏ&

When was the last time you woke up and realized that today could be the best day of your life?

&ᴏ&

ༀༀ

Stop allowing other people to dilute or poison your day with their words or opinions. Stand strong in the truth of your beauty and journey through your day without attachment to the validation of others.

ༀༀ

Let today be the day you finally release yourself from the imprisonment of past grudges and anger. Simplify your life. Let go of the poisonous past and live the abundantly beautiful present... today.

ༀༀ

Free yourself from the limitations you placed upon yourself. There is no-thing holding you back.

ༀༀ

It's not always what we don't know that gets in our way; sometimes it's what we think we know that keeps us from learning.

ༀༀ

CHANGE: Don't just talk about it, go out there and do it. Don't just meditate about it, go out there and create it. Don't just pray about it, go out there and take action; participate in the answering of your own prayer. If you want change, get out there and live it.

ༀༀ

If You Want to Learn How to Live, Hang Out with People Who Are Dying

I have spent many years as a volunteer at veterans' hospitals; often spending the final days with our brothers and sisters who have served. I must say, there is nobody as free as somebody who is dying. Conversations are usually pure uncensored truth from someone who has nothing to lose.

I am often asked how I have accomplished so much at a young age and how I continue to multi-task between businesses and working passionately towards my dreams. My answer is always that I have learned how to effectively live from the advice of those who are dying.

Even though the veterans I have sat with were different ages, from different walks of life, and of varying spiritual and religious backgrounds, they always gave a personal version of a common ideal; to live my life to the max.

They fervently insist that I pursue my dreams; that I love unapologetically; that I forgive mercifully; that I share with others; that I take chances; that I accept my faults; that I find humor in life; that I stress less; that I give hugs; that I chase the girl of my dreams; that I leave work at the office; that I watch what I eat;

that I respect others; that I learn and explore; that I appreciate what I have; that I live each day to its fullest.

I remember one particular conversation that had a really deep impact on me. I was sitting with an older veteran; I had been visiting him for several months and had built a good rapport with him. The gentleman and I were speaking about life and the opportunities it gives us. He said, "When I was young, I thought I was invincible and that I would live forever. My ideas of living forever made me miss out on living in each day. I didn't see or appreciate all of the opportunities I had. I kept postponing my own dreams because I felt I had an eternity to fulfill them. Now I realize that I'm not invincible and I can't believe that I talked myself out of living; I talked myself out of chasing my dreams."

I will never forget those words, "I talked myself out of living; I talked myself out of chasing my dreams."

I realized then, that this man, this former soldier, this former business dynamo, this dad, this grandpa, this withered man, with his wrinkled hands and weathered face, is me; he is ALL of us. We do that to ourselves all the time.

How many times have you talked yourself out of living? How many times have you talked yourself out of taking a chance? How many times have you talked yourself out of chasing your dreams?

How would your life be different if you stopped talking yourself out of living the life you have dreamt of?

My life is a reflection of what I have learned from these transitioning souls.

I am aware that my time is limited. I am aware that my moment is now. My moment to love, my moment to give, my moment to achieve, my moment to forgive, my moment to endeavor, my moment to follow my dreams... my moment is NOW. I refuse to live with the regret of gambling for tomorrow. I will not lay on my deathbed wondering what might have been. I will ride the waves of purpose and chance towards the wonderful splendor of my dreams. At the end of my day, I will rest my head on the pillow of a day well-lived and a life well-ventured.

Red Carpet Events:

Sitting on the couch and watching people who actually chase their goals and dreams; criticizing what they're wearing... and wondering why we're depressed.

ഔരു

Ideas and philosophies have a shelf-life. They must be kept fresh and renewed or they will spoil. If left unattended, the same ideas and philosophies that once nourished you and helped you grow can poison you and make you sick. Become aware of new ideas that can refresh your way of life and be open to the fact that your old ideas and philosophies can work for you for some time, but when the shelf-life has passed, those ideas and philosophies could also harm you.

ഔരു

Free yourself from the burden of feeling the need to hold on to anything. Let go... you are a part of everything.

ഔരു

Happiness, after all, is found in the simplest of things.

ഔരു

Sometimes letting go is simply changing the labels you place on an event. Looking at the same event with fresh eyes.

ഔരു

Why are we so quick to limit the possibility of our own happiness?

ഔരു

৪৩

It's up to you today to start making healthy choices. Not choices that are just healthy for your body, but healthy for your mind.

৪৩

Many great ideas, great love stories, and great achievements are born from a healthy irrationality.

৪৩

Shake things up. Do something different. Take planned, calculated steps towards a new goal, or a new you. It's the only way to ensure that you won't get the same results in your life.

৪৩

As soon as you start feeding yourself better emotionally, spiritually, and physically, everything responds in the positive.

৪৩

It is an unnecessary burden to make negative judgmental assumptions about others. We are all on a journey.

৪৩

Notes to my Younger Self

Most people have an abundance
of dreams, but lack the courage
to follow them. Help them find
that courage by inspiring them
with yours.

My Own Greatest Hero, My Own Worst Enemy

Your life is a story you're telling yourself. I like to live each day of my life as if it's a page, a chapter in my life's story. I get to choose how my story plays out. Even if I don't get to choose the events that happen, I do get to choose the labels I place on the events and what role I play in this story.

When I'm the hero of my story: I see opportunities, I feel gratitude, I am inspired by choices, I am emotionally strong, I am physically relentless, and I am aware and conscious to place empowering labels on the events that occur throughout my day. For me, this system of mindful choice-making as the author of my story has led to tremendous levels of success.

Are you the hero of your own story? If you are not the hero of your own story, then you're missing the whole point of your humanity. Maybe the hero that is missing from your story is you. When you become the hero of your own story, you activate a power within you to make changes to your entire life.

Whether consciously or unconsciously, we are all the authors of our own story. Too many people play a victim role or spend each day writing in the same things that caused them stress the day before. They keep themselves surrounded by the same disempowering or drama-filled characters and rarely make the mindful choice to change the story. Sometimes people even let others write their story for them. This leads to a feeling of helplessness and hopelessness; the opposite of your design.

Today is a new day! You have the opportunity to pick up life's pen and change your story. Become the hero; the greatest hero in your story, and you'll see how much more exciting your life will be. You will watch your goals and dreams transition from something you simply hoped for to something within your powerful grasp.

Remember, life itself is simple; it's just not easy. Each new day is a day that no one has ever seen... a blank page in your story. What are you going to do with it? What will this page say? Will it be a story of a hero... a powerful story... a redemptive story... what will it be? Only YOU get to choose.

When you judge a woman by her appearance, it doesn't define her, it defines you. Ladies, never allow yourself to be defined by someone's inability to appreciate your unique beauty.

೫೦೦೪

You have been blessed with immeasurable power to make positive changes in your life.

೫೦೦೪

Focusing on what you don't want instead of focusing on what you do want gets you nowhere. Negativity makes a horrible motivator. Decide what you want and move in that direction.

೫೦೦೪

Free yourself from fruitlessly worrying about things you can't control and put your energy towards the things you can. Seize the day and take effective action on things you can change.

೫೦೦೪

Stop validating your victim mentality. Shake off your self-defeating drama and embrace your innate ability to recover and achieve.

೫೦೦೪

Walk away from gossip and verbal defamation. Speak only the good you know of other people and encourage others to do the same.

೫೦೦೪

What we call consciousness is our ability to perceive stimuli and to file it within the parameters of our personal story.

೫೦೦೪

෩෨

Incredible change happens in your life when you decide to take control of what you do have power over instead of craving control over what you don't.

෩෨

Change is in the air. This change reminds us that we are made and beautifully sculpted by the same power that orchestrates the change of season. Let this be the season you embrace and align yourself with this change.

෩෨

What are you waiting for? How long will you keep waiting? Don't sit back and wait for life to happen to you. Have a plan and take the needed steps to create what you want.

෩෨

The art of letting go is simply about personal empowerment. Realizing what you're in charge of, realizing what you control, and more importantly, what you don't control.

෩෨

Give freely, love fully, and play feverously! Don't put so many conditioned rules on your happiness. Life can be a beautiful experience if we allow it.

෩෨

Your Whole Life is Ahead of You

I can't even count the amount of times an older person has told me, "You've got your whole life ahead of you." Upon hearing these words intended to provide comforting advice, one can't help but feel the older person is latently implying that they do not; that they are actually saying, "I'm old now, but you've got your whole life ahead of you."

While it is easy to understand, and even feel, like your glory days have passed, the truth is that no matter how old you are, your life isn't behind you, your memories are behind you. Your life is always ahead of you. From this moment, right now, you have just as much opportunity as anybody else to make decisions and take actions that will propel you towards the life you want.

No matter where you are or what you're doing, no matter how old you are, or what you've been through, no matter how many times you've been delayed, hurt, or back-stabbed, please remember that your whole life is ahead of you. What is left behind you are life-moments that have expired; we call them "memories" and they continue to exists in your mind. Your vibrant and enhance-able life is what flows before you now.

Folks, don't let your expired life-moments nourish your journey of today. It's easy to tell ourselves a story of disempowerment; that the youth of today are the only ones with their life ahead of them. But the truth is, as we all open our eyes to this new day, we awaken to the same potentiality; the same opportunity to live life to its greatest potential.

How would your life be different if you lived accordingly and stopped telling yourself the lie that your best days are behind you?

There is magic in this wonderful life, but only if you choose to do more than just exist; the magic is found when we choose to live.

ഇരു

Be consistent in your dedication to showing your gratitude to others. Gratitude is fuel, medicine, and spiritual and emotional nourishment.

ഇരു

Your life begins to change the day you take responsibility for it.

ഇരു

Are you going to allow the world around you to change while you remain stagnant? Make this the time you throw away old habits that have hindered your happiness and success and finally allow your greatest self to flourish.

ഇരു

Your capacity to experience the fullness of life is directly proportionate to your capacity to experience the fullness of love.

ഇരു

A healthy choice for your overall health and well-being is one of a happy and positive disposition.

ഇരു

There is a distinct feeling of contentment that engulfs your entire being after a day well lived, a battle well fought, and a purpose tirelessly pursued.

ഇരു

Notes to my Younger Self

Sports Jerseys: To wear another man's name on your back is a subconscious slap in the face to who you are. Don't fantasize about being someone else. Put in the work required to rise to the level of your greatest self.

The Journey's Baggage

I am a people watcher and I travel a lot. At times, this makes for entertainment, aggravation, and even observational learning. On one particular occasion, I was coming back to New York from a business trip out west. The plane landed and I couldn't wait to get to my car and go home. As I walked through the airport like a man on a mission, breezing past baggage claim, I couldn't help but hear the excited cheers of young kids.

Curiosity caused me to look in the direction of these extremely loud and excited kids. It appeared to me that their dad had come home from a trip. These kids were jumping up and down in excitement and as soon as their dad got close to them, they tackled his legs – even as a distant observer, it was a pretty touching moment.

The dad seemed equally happy to see his kids as he looked down at them hugging his legs and jumping at him as he tried his best to hold his arms high and not to hit the kids with the luggage in his hands.

The excitement was touching and gained the attention of several people in the area as the kids were yelling for him to pick them up. As I watched, I was thinking to myself that he can't pick them, he can't embrace them, he can't receive the love they're sharing until he lets go of the luggage; the baggage he was holding from his trip.

And again, I couldn't help but liken that to all of our lives. This man could not embrace what the NOW had to offer while he was holding on to the luggage from his journey.

How many of us walk around being weighted down by the baggage of our journey? You can't possibly embrace that new relationship, that new companion, that new career, that new friendship, or that new life you want while you're still holding on to the baggage of the last one. Let go... and allow yourself to embrace what is waiting for you right at your feet.

> Let today be the day you finally stop having a conflict between your actions and your goals. When you align your greatest intent with purposeful action, you create a universal symphony serenading your success!

ॐ

Stop wasting your time looking for the key to happiness... the door is open and unlocked... just walk through it.

ॐ

Most people are resentful of the happiness of others and yet we seem to seek validation from others in order to allow our own happiness... it's easy to see the problem with this system.

ॐ

Life is a treasure-chest of opportunities, choices, and time. Unfortunately, the choice many people make is to argue about the details of the chest instead of seizing the treasure within it.

ॐ

I used to hold grudges until I realized that most people are narcissistic and their actions are driven by an unhealthy self-interest and not maliciousness towards me.

ॐ

Change is nature's way of offering us the opportunity to explore the parameters of our humanity and potential. Don't fight it, embrace it. There is a magical experience awaiting those who embrace this natural process.

ॐ

၆၁၈

We can spend today joyously celebrating potential by acting upon our purpose, or we can spend it mourning the days and opportunities gone by... the first will find you amongst the few who are content and accomplished; the latter will find you with the suffering majority as you exhaustedly swim in the ocean of regret.

၆၁၈

If you argue with reality, you will only cause yourself pain. However if you accept reality and build on it, the things you create will be durable, true, and healing.

၆၁၈

Remember when your curiosity inspired your investigative mind to explore and learn... you weren't bogged down with resentment, cynicism, and emotional baggage... just think about how great it would be to return to that mindset of unencumbered learning and adventurous living... you are just one choice away from that life... choose to let go of the infertile past... go live your adventure!

၆၁၈

If we could see a graph of how much pain and limitation we cause in our own lives through the lies we tell ourselves, we would immediately eliminate this nasty habit.

၆၁၈

Happiness in Simplicity

I'm not sure why some people choose to engulf themselves in a drama filled life, but they do. And for some reason, they feel they should allow me to partake in their drama buffet. No thanks!

I learned a long time ago that there is stress in the complex and happiness in the simple. The "growing" we attribute to becoming more mature, in finding our happy place, could be more accurately described as "shrinking," as we cut away the nonsense that emotionally weighs us down.

How would your life be different if you cut away the people who try to pull you in to their drama filled lives? What drama could you cut away from your own life?

There have been extensive studies on how the stress caused by drama has negative effects on our lives and our bodies. Love yourself enough to break this cycle... Love yourself enough to take the actions required for your happiness... Love yourself enough to cut yourself loose from the ties of the drama-filled past... Love yourself enough to move on!

Happiness is found in the simplest of things. Happiness is found in gratitude, in a kept promise, in a good conversation, in love, in friendship, in an achieved goal, in a fond memory; in all the simple magnificence of life.

Be free of the complexities of drama. Be free of those who live it and those who share it. You've been around long enough to see it can never be helpful; cut it away! Like the plaque on my office wall says, "Save the drama for your momma."

Happiness is not a thing to be achieved but it is a thing to be experienced; it's a way of life. It is a choice one makes to love one's self enough to live in gratitude without accepting the devilish invitation to complicate things.

Choose happiness today!

Today you will have countless opportunities to take action towards any dream or goal you've ever had. No matter how long you've waited, it's never too late. Let today be the day you give life to your dreams and goals.

೮೦೮ෆ

Let go of the people who dull your shine, poison your spirit, and bring you drama. Cancel your subscription to their issues.

೮೦೮ෆ

By surrounding yourself with people who are positive, caring, intelligent, loving, and open-minded, you create a personal environment that is conducive to your emotional and personal growth. By surrounding yourself with the opposite, you create a personal environment that is conducive to the opposite.

೮೦೮ෆ

Can you hold happiness? Can you drink it? Can you taste it? Can you touch it? Of course not, it is immaterial. So, stop looking for it in the material world! Happiness is experienced within; when we bridge the gap between what we want to experience and how we choose to behave.

೮೦೮ෆ

Instructions for successful living: Dream it. Plan it. Do it. Repeat.

೮೦೮ෆ

There is no greater symphony of self-destruction than the beautifully poisonous melody found in our excuses.

೮೦೮ෆ

శు

Fear waters the weeds of regret.

శు

Do you think peace of mind can be found in holding a grudge... or harboring resentment... or wallowing in thoughts of what could have been? Me neither.

శు

If you are bored, you're doing yourself a tremendous disservice. Open your mind, break-free from your conditioned routine, and reignite the flames of excitement and discovery.

శు

When I was young, I used to wish I would fit in... I'm glad I didn't get my wish.

శు

Your ability to see beauty and possibility is proportionate to the level at which you embrace gratitude.

శు

Self-love isn't always so poetic; sometimes it's a nice big triple back flip kick in the ass. You've got to call yourself on your own nonsense; on the incredibly efficient way you can be self-destructive.

శు

Notes to my Younger Self

Set a high standard on how you treat women. Whether they appreciate it or not, don't lower your own standards of behavior.

Love

&

Relationships...

Set the Standard

How do you feel when you walk into someone's house and it looks well-organized and pristinely clean? You immediately feel the need to kick off your shoes at the door and it doesn't occur to you to eat on the couch or to make a mess in any way.

Do you feel the same urge of impeccable behavior when you walk into someone's house and it's dirty or a mess? Of course not; there is no need to.

You see, without saying a word, but simply by their behavior and lifestyle, the homeowners have set a standard for how you will respect them and their space. By their actions, they have communicated a standard for how they want to be treated.

It's easy to see this system of setting standards when applied to our homes but it is less simple, although equally true, to see how this same system affects our relationships.

What relationship standards are your behaviors and actions setting?

Do you love yourself, respect yourself, and treat yourself in a pristine respectable manner; inspiring others to do the same? Or do you break promises to yourself, not care for your health, not forgive yourself, and not show yourself respect; inspiring others to do the same?

What standard are you setting?

Many people make the mistake of expecting others to treat them in a more loving and respectful way than they treat themselves. If you don't love yourself, stop expecting others to. If you don't respect yourself, stop expecting others to. If you don't keep promises to yourself, stop expecting others to. If you are not faithful to your dreams, your goals, and your resolutions, stop expecting others to be.

We inspire others to treat us by the way we treat ourselves. The most important relationship you will ever have is the one with yourself. It is in this relationship that we set the standard for all others.

●　　●　　●

Love moves in sync with the cadence of forgiveness, sings in tune with the melody of acceptance, and dances in rhythm with the music of companionship.

●　　●　　●

഼ഽ

Service and gratitude will fuel your relationship; entitlement and expectation will poison it.

഼ഽ

I knew you were the one when I realized your smile was my heaven, your laugh my favorite song, and your arms my home.

഼ഽ

Forever is a measure of time used by people who share an ordinary love. Our extraordinary love is immeasurable... for us, forever just won't do.

഼ഽ

If you want drama, settle for the one who will change your relationship status. If you want love, wait for the one who will change your life.

഼ഽ

I will not try to convince you to love me, to respect me, to commit to me. I deserve better than that; I AM BETTER THAN THAT... Goodbye.

഼ഽ

You didn't just cheat on me; you cheated on us. You didn't just break my heart; you broke our future.

഼ഽ

Relationships: If you put up with it, you're going to end up with it. Set the standard you want and don't settle for less.

Nourishing Relationships

Relationships challenge us; they always have and always will. There is a constant conflict between the common relationship dynamic and our innate narcissistic needs. It seems this attempt to find a healthy balance in our relationships often causes an emotional and manifested tug of war. This leads us to lose sight of how to nourish our relationships.

If you want to strengthen your relationship, remember this: Our relationships, whether business or personal, are nourished and shaped by the commitment we express through our actions.

Break-free from the relationship-poisoning mindset of narcissism! Don't be a taker; healthy relationships require balance. Give with your words and be extra generous with your deeds. Remember, while words can be powerful, eloquent, and lasting, it is our committed action that will ultimately serve as the defining factor of our relationships. If you make a conscious effort to ensure your words are in alignment with your actions, you can be confident that you will build strong relationships with others who do the same.

⮘⮙

Only insecure boys will belittle a woman. The greatest way to "man-up" is to empower women.

⮘⮙

Our love is perfect. And even though we may not be, our love creates a bridge that spans over our imperfections and joins us where it matters.

⮘⮙

My relationship stays strong because I serenade her with my actions... and I write poetry in her heart with my deeds. My endless love is expressed with more than just my words; my love is lived as a verb.

⮘⮙

The strength of a man isn't seen in the power of his arms. It's seen in the love with which he EMBRACES you.

⮘⮙

Sometimes it's the same moments that take your breath away that breathe purpose and love back into your life.

⮘⮙

Meeting you was not the first day of the rest of my life; it was the first day of the BEST of my life.

⮘⮙

Notes to my Younger Self

Let your handshake be a greater
bond than any written contract.

Where it Matters

Being with you today is worth all the broken hearts of yesterday. In a flash, all of the stumbling blocks of relationships gone wrong have become the stepping stones to our perfect love.

We fit. I now understand the feeling I used to think was pain that came along with love was actually the discomfort from being in a place I didn't fit.

Thank you for being you... for sharing your love with me... for inspiring me to accept myself... for helping me see the unique beauty in imperfection... for showing me that love is something you do; something not just to be said, but also to be shown.

I am not perfect; neither are you. I love that!

Our love is perfect. And even though we may not be, our love creates a bridge that spans over our imperfections and joins us where it matters.

I love you!

ഓൽ

Our relationships are nourished and shaped by the commitment we express through our actions. Don't just speak; ACT!

ഓൽ

When you finally meet the right one for you, it suddenly becomes clear why everyone else was so wrong.

ഓൽ

I'm not crying because of you; you're not worth it. I'm crying because my delusion of who you were was shattered by the truth of who you are.

ഓൽ

Love is forgiving, accepting, moving on, embracing, and all encompassing. And if you're not doing that for yourself, you cannot do that with anyone else.

ഓൽ

I believe in the immeasurable power of love; that true love can endure any circumstance and reach across any distance.

ഓൽ

There are not enough days in forever to allow me to fully express the depth of my love for you.

ഓൽ

She lives her life like a flame; a dance of purposeful chaos. Her enchanting light can guide you and quell your fears... She's hot; warming those who respect her and burning those who don't... She's a flame with an unforgettable glow... A weak man will try to dim her luminance... But her soul mate will take pleasure in fanning the blaze.

Batshit Kind of Love

The type of love that can't be described with words...

The type of love that can't be measured by time...

The type of love that inspires haters to hate...

The type of love that makes no sense to those around you...

The type of love that exists in the beautiful eyes in which you can see all of your tomorrows... all of your children and grandchildren...

The type of love that makes you feel like forever will not be long enough...

The type of love that is born out of a relationship that is built on honor, respect, and truth...

That is our love... That is our connection...

The batshit kind of love that makes no sense at all... and at the same time... all the sense in the world...

That is us...

You and me; a "WE."

જી૦ભ

A broken heart bleeds tears.

જી૦ભ

A beautiful thing happens when we start paying attention to each other. It is by participating more in your relationship that you breathe life into it.

જી૦ભ

Being in a relationship doesn't entitle you to anything. You don't get what you expect, you get what you create.

જી૦ભ

Love encompasses so much, reaches so far, and heals so deeply, that any attempt to describe it, no matter how poetic, only dilutes it.

જી૦ભ

My soul feels reborn each time I see you; falling in love with you again and again.

જી૦ભ

As your insecurity becomes nourished our relationship becomes poisoned.

જી૦ભ

YOU are your love of a lifetime.

જી૦ભ

Notes to my Younger Self

Learn to say "please" and "thank you" in multiple languages.

When Forever Becomes A Place

Forever is used as a reference of time; but there are not enough days in forever to allow me to fully express the depth of my love for you.

Perhaps it is enough time for those who share an ordinary love. But not us; our extraordinary love is immeasurable... for us, forever just won't do.

I prefer to think of forever as a place...

When forever becomes a place... when forever ceases to be just a word... when it ceases to be just a measurement of time... but instead becomes a place where soul mates can dance to the song in their hearts; that is a reflection of true love... that is our love.

I feel so blessed to share this forever with you. To love, share, laugh, grow, dance, learn, and play along this journey through forever. This is our home, our place; forever.

ဆာလ

If you're not comfortable enough with yourself or with your own truth when entering a relationship, then you're not ready for that relationship.

ဆာလ

It is love's nature to be expressed.

ဆာလ

When love is at the base of something, it is a masterpiece.

ဆာလ

The greatest love stories are not those in which love is only spoken, but those in which it is acted upon.

ဆာလ

Being close but feeling far, talking but not being heard, loving but not being loved, that is the painful reality of a dying relationship.

ဆာလ

Sometimes the comfort of being in a relationship lulls you into mundane complacency; you become irrelevant in each other's lives. We call this phenomenon "growing apart."

ဆာလ

When in a relationship, a real man doesn't make his woman jealous of others; he makes others jealous of his woman.

I Love Loving You

You are my favorite song; a rhythm of beauty that captures my spirit.

You are my favorite poem; an exquisite grouping of ideas set in motion with an unmatched enchanting elegance.

You are my best friend; from our laughter to our deep conversations, our moments together are a timeless pleasure.

You are my soul mate; a connection so pure, so powerful, that it can only be considered divine.

You are my lover; a passionate entwinement, a chorus of ecstasy, and a feeling of complete unity that words could never adequately describe.

You are my angel; you remind me of the goodness in this world and inspire me to be the greatest version of myself.

You are my home; it is in your loving gaze that I find the comfort, acceptance, and the sense of belonging.

You are my love ~ mi amor; there are not enough days in forever to allow me to fully express my love for you.

I love loving you.

෨෬

Do not sabotage your new relationship with your last relationship's poison.

෨෬

I find the best way to love someone is not to change them, but instead, help them reveal the greatest version of themselves.

෨෬

By reacting from fear instead of responding from love, you inject poison directly into the veins of your relationship.

෨෬

I feel so blessed to discover that in each new day, I have the opportunity to watch the sunrise and fall in love with you again.

෨෬

Let's agree to be honest from the start. I would rather feel the disappointment that comes with the realization that we are incompatible than to feel the pain and betrayal that comes with finding out that we're full of crap.

෨෬

Gratitude is nutrition for a living relationship.

෨෬

Notes to my Younger Self

There are some people who will
never see you as being good
enough. That is their short-coming
not yours. Be merciful enough
to yourself to cut them out
of your life.

Let's Not Forget

Our love is beyond the confines of time... timeless... shapeless... formless... a beautiful dance between uniquely designed souls... fitting as one...

As we grow in our love... let's not forget that we are also growing as individuals... each bringing new dimensions to our relationship... let's respect each other's journey...

As we grow in our family... let's not forget that we, as a couple, still need attention... let's not lose grip of the excitement of our flirtation and our passion for each other... while we tend to the "we," let's not forget the "us"...

As we grow in age... let's not forget that our souls are age-less and we still have youthful dreams and wishes... let's keep conversations open and free... keeping an updated version of each other... let's not forget that the greatest love stories are nourished in great friendship... we shall keep our love and friendship strong...

Through all the challenges life may throw at us; let's not forget that we are soul mates... companions... individuals... divinely fused together by the immeasurable power of love... and that we can get through it all... as one.

ౚఴ

My love for you spans over the lines of my past, present, and future. You are what I love remembering, what I love experiencing, and what I love looking forward to.

ౚఴ

When the world makes me feel like I am alone, love reminds me otherwise.

ౚఴ

Life is too short to not kick fear in the ass and allow yourself to love again.

ౚఴ

There is something innocently beautiful about watching two people behave as though no one else existed, and lovingly act silly together.

ౚఴ

Cheaters are cowards that are tempted to chase the fantasy of what could be... instead of courageously addressing their own self-destructive behavior and cultivating what is.

ౚఴ

Our love is sharpened by the stone of our challenges and strengthened by the struggles of our growth.

ౚఴ

♥ ♥ ♥ ♥ ♥ ♥
She is delightfully
chaotic; a beautiful
mess. Loving her is a
splendid adventure.
♥ ♥ ♥ ♥ ♥ ♥

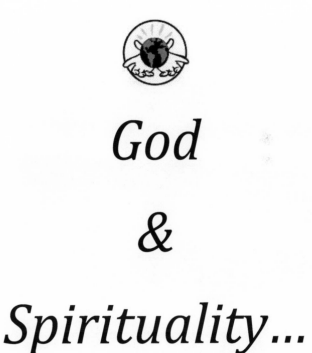

God

&

Spirituality...

Don't Confuse Religion for God

What are we doing? Instead of being nice, instead of being compassionate to each other, instead of helping each other, we are judging each other for our beliefs. That isn't faithfulness to a God. That is faithfulness to a religion. It is clear that we have come to a point where we confuse a religion for God.

We have confused the story for the message. We get caught up in the details of our differing theistic stories and we argue, often violently, the details of these stories instead of honoring the common message.

We see this played out in our wars. We see this played out in disputes in our communities. We see it played out in our domestic and international policies. Our relationships are damaged, our families split, our nations torn, and our minds confused because we have all become conditioned to be more faithful to a religion, and the story in the particular religion, than to the message of the God. In essence, we have been taught to worship the religion instead of the God.

Religions vary. Characters in the theistic stories vary. Time, place, and languages vary. Throughout the world's recorded history, many religions have held prominent roles in their respective societies; and even though the details of each story may vary, the message of the story has always been the same.

174 | Unapologetically You

Be loving. Be forgiving. Be compassionate. Be kind. Share with others. Treat people as you want to be treated.

Why don't we focus our religious enthusiasm on these wonderful messages instead of fighting about the details of our differing stories? Why do we treat our religious designations with the same blind and belligerent loyalty as we do our favorite sports teams?

For thousands of years, from wars to science denial to slavery to rape to mandated inequality; the sustained influence of religious dogma has left a polarizing effect on the global population. But in this heated debate, let's not convict the message of God for crimes committed by the ravenous guidelines of theistic dogma.

Religions are born from the stories of a people's subjective experience of God. The expression and devotion of religion's followers isn't always negative. There have been many beautiful works done in the name of religion. And while the subjective experience of God holds personal value, it is important to not lose sight of the objective reality that religion can be good – it can even be great; but it can never be God. As a global society, we would take a magnificent step towards peace and harmony to not confuse the two.

୫୦୦୫

Religion is the subjective experience. Science is the objective reality. To argue either is a ridiculous waste of time and energy.

୫୦୦୫

In every religious and sacred text, faith is a verb; a thing to be demonstrated. It is in modern days that we have diluted faith from an act to a philosophy.

୫୦୦୫

Just because I don't believe in YOUR God doesn't mean I don't believe in God. I just choose not to be bound by the limits of your imagination or those of your ancestors.

୫୦୦୫

If I told you to wish for good health, you would think I'm ridiculous; but when I exchange the word "wish" for the word "pray," you believe it can work. That is the disempowering delusion religions have brought us.

୫୦୦୫

Want to keep Christ in Christmas? Feed the hungry, clothe the naked, forgive the guilty, welcome the unwanted, care for the ill, love your enemies, and do unto others as you would have done unto you.

୫୦୦୫

God is the composer; you are the song.

୫୦୦୫

If the universe does consist of a battle between the devil and God, the final analysis should conclude that religion would have been the devil's most brilliant move... and science, God's.

Love is My Religion

Love is a way of life. Love is open. Love is undefined. Love is infinite. Love cannot be weighed. It cannot be measured. It cannot be put on a graph. Love is all-encompassing yet incalculable. Sometimes it will take over your whole life. It will be in every breath, in every blink, in every step, in every word, in every thought, and engulf your entire being with its intangible abundance.

For me, love is my religion. It is the foundation of my church. It is the guideline of my creed. It is the song of my prayer. It does not condemn. It does not judge. It does not betray. It does not begrudge. It does not war.

When you live in alignment with love; great things happen. Love will fuel the hero and will defuse the villain. It is an endless well of spiritual and emotional nourishment. Love will forgive, heal, inspire, embrace, and transform your life.

Love is my religion.

৪৩

Life may bring you to your knees; pray. Then GET UP and participate in the answer. BECOME the remedy! BE the solution!

৪৩

Don't tell me about your God with your words. Show me about your God with your actions.

৪৩

No matter what your sacred or religious book is, it's not how well you know the book; it's how well you're in alignment with the author.

৪৩

There is no humility in calling yourself a Christian; placing Christ in the role of colleague. The humility lies in the truth of your imperfection and a more accurate description as a student of Christianity; placing Christ back in the role as head teacher.

৪৩

Sometimes in the quest for enlightenment the only thing that gets lighter is your wallet.

৪৩

Sometimes not getting what you want is God's greatest blessing.

৪৩

Notes to my Younger Self

Don't let your idea of God be
limited to the imagination of
others. Don't let them define your
God and don't let them tell you
how to express your faith.

Masters, and Preachers, and Gurus, Oh My!

We are nonphysical, spiritual consciousness experiencing a material human existence. In the scope of eternity, we are spiritual beings that spend a very short time living this human experience. You are already a spiritual being; always have been – always will be. Why would you throw away even a single human day, trying to be what you already are? And why would any of us succumb to the parasitic antics of the countless "Masters" and "Preachers" and "Gurus"... oh my?!?

For years, centuries, and millennia we have had these masters and preachers and gurus (oh my) trying to teach us to be something we already are. We are enchanted by their charismatic and pain-anesthetizing words, but during this process, we lose connection with our human potentiality. So we end up with plenty of spiritual solutions to deal with our stressful human feelings, but no practical strategies to avoid those feelings and situations to begin with.

We end up buying these books in the Spiritual, Self-Help, Personal Growth sections of the book store (notice these sections get bigger and bigger). We attend the huge expo events, with masters and preachers and gurus speaking and peddling their "miracle" products; talking about transcending your humanity and liberating yourself from the material world... while charging you very real human money for their products and services.

Life is challenging. We have money issues, relationship issues, health issues, personal issues, professional issues, etc... So of course these charismatic orators and brilliant marketers have success selling us their "solution" or "secret" or "salvation" to our problems. But we fail to see that we get caught up in a cycle of needing their anesthesia instead of just confronting the issue that causes us the problems to begin with.

You have problems paying bills? That's not a spiritual problem, it's a financial one. Stop looking elsewhere for the solution and DEAL with it. If you're having relationship issues, that's not a spiritual problem. Get your head out of the clouds and put it back into the parameters of your partnership. DEAL with your communication issues, or maturity issues, or friendship issues, don't seek an answer from a source that was not the issue to begin with. You are already a spiritual being... you have been created with every tool you need to remedy your situations and live your purpose... anyone who tells you different either lacks an understanding of the depth of our existence and potentiality, or is trying to sell you something (or both).

You don't have a spiritual problem, or a mystical energy problem, or a prayer problem, or meditation problem; what you have is a very human problem that can only be fixed in a very human way. While spiritual techniques can offer amazing relief for such life stresses, they cannot solve the cause of the stress. The reason we see more masters and preachers and gurus (oh my) come into the commercial world, and we watch the associated sections of the book stores grow and grow, is because they figured out an effective way to offer a simple cure to a problem we don't have... and we fall for it 100% of the time.

If you want true change in your life, you MUST take responsibility. Embrace the truth that your spirituality wasn't the cause of your stress and it's not going to be the solution either. If you want something different, you must live differently. Incorporate a healthy balance of your spirituality and humanity. Pray, meditate, visualize; then get up and take actions that will bring them to life. Pray, meditate, visualize for better finances; then make better financial decisions. Pray, meditate, visualize for better relationships; then make mature, love-driven decisions. Pray, meditate, visualize for a healthier life; then exercise and make better food choices. LIVE your prayer, ACT on your meditation, BE your visualization.

How would your life be different if you finally let go of your need to be validated or nourished by the preachers and masters and gurus (oh my); and finally looked at yourself in the mirror and said, "I'm going to breathe life back into my life. I'm going to take responsibility, I'm going to take action, and I'm going to live my life, my prayer, my meditation, my faith, and my dreams as a VERB!" Let today be the day you embrace your spirituality without turning your back on your humanity. Squeeze this amazing human experience for all of its nourishing juices. Take action towards the life you see for yourself. Don't just look to the sky and beg for it; put your feet on the ground and create it! You are more powerful than you know! Explore the depth of that power today!

How would your life be different if your religion was love, and your spirituality was governed by kindness? How would the world be different if everyone did this?

184 | *Unapologetically You*

Prayer is inward communication with yourself; action is outward conversation with God.

ℬℭ

God is the name we give to the science we don't understand. Science is the name we give to the God we don't understand.

ℬℭ

It has been my experience that those who claim to be the most spiritual are usually the least so.

ℬℭ

Through my choices and actions, I have learned the most effective way of speaking to God is without saying a word.

ℬℭ

When you're too religious, you tend to point your finger to judge instead of extending your hand to help.

ℬℭ

Jesus said "Give us THIS DAY our daily bread," knowing that you cannot fight today's battles with yesterday's bread. Knowing that you cannot fight today's battles with the hope of tomorrow's bread. Knowing that today you will be nourished by this daily bread, and it's what you have to fight today's battle.

ℬℭ

When I look back, I realize I was praying for something God had already given me.

Mom on the Eighth Floor

It was a year from her diagnosis to her death. Mom was a dynamic, classy, beautiful woman; always sharing her vibrant laughter and contagious smile. She and dad had been married since she was a teenager. They put their whole heart and soul into creating the life they dreamed of; and even though she was still young, they had planned to eventually retire and travel.

Cancer had a different plan.

Instead, we spent a year in and out of the hospital as she battled this unmerciful devil. Watching as it slowly and methodically consumed my 57 year old mom and her future. That year of hospital visits seemed like an entire lifetime. That eighth floor would not only serve as a place where mom's amazing doctors and nurses would treat her; not only as the place she would take her last breath, but also as the place she would come to inspire all of us with her grace, strength, courage, and unconditional love.

Mom was only 5 feet tall. I used to laugh that I was the same height as her while I was still in elementary school. She married my dad when she was still a teenager and together, having both been raised in poverty, they moved from Chile to the USA with the intention of building a better life for themselves and their children.

And what a life they built! Her heavily attended funeral caused the shut-down of the main roads in our Long Island town. So many people from so many places came to pay their respect to this incredible woman I was blessed to call mom. Kind words from countless people sharing stories on how mom helped them was a reflection of her generous heart, honest wisdom, and unselfish spirit.

As for me, a normally loving person, during that year on the eighth floor, I had come to hate cancer. I hated the cancer for its cruelty and merciless nature... I hated this heartless enemy for not showing compassion or sympathy... I hated this evil cancer for putting us all through an emotionally laborious hell with no payoff but more sadness... I hated cancer.

For mom, I can only imagine the horror of this process. There are so many ups and downs, seemingly archaic tests and treatments, and plenty of time for contemplation and tears. You often hear the terms "Battle" and "Fight" attributed to this nasty grueling process. A year in and out of the eighth floor had taken its toll on all of us.

One day, mom taught us all such a great lesson: You win 100% of every fight you DON'T engage in. She decided that instead of losing the battle with cancer, with the same elegance and grace she had been known for, she would politely excuse herself from the

188 | Unapologetically You

process. What a beautiful day that was! Mom decided that instead of dying on cancer's terms, she would LIVE on her own.

While the strength she showed during that year was nothing short of incredible and miraculous, it was her wisdom that would have the final say... and inspire us all.

On that wonderful day, the stressed out patient was gone and we got mom back. She was happy, laughing, joking, giving orders, saying "I love you" every chance she got; she was FREE! She said, "I don't want to live like I'm dying... I want to live like I'm living!"

During that year, in my private time with mom, we shared so many memories, love, and laughter. We talked about life and she would often explain to me what she was feeling and how the process of dying gave her so much clarity on spirituality and God. We talked about the after-life and what this life had meant to her. She spoke to me as a mom, a friend, a mentor, and a fellow observer. Her insight was captivating, inspiring, and life-changing.

Our last conversation was about what she wanted from me after she was gone. Amongst the simple things she wanted me to do was to make sure my dad, the love of her life, and my brother and sister were always ok. She also spoke to me about the days immediately ahead; perhaps her final great lesson for me. She said, "I know you'll give a good talk at my funeral, but I want you to make sure you keep it positive and talk about the blessings this cancer brought us."

As you can imagine, this request by my mom was a tough task. How does one speak well of cancer?

I wasn't sure what I was going to say. I still hated cancer with a passion. It had killed my mom. It had stolen her future and broken the heart of everyone who loved her. Cancer was my enemy.

As I stood there at our local church, in the same spot my mom and dad had recently made a special trip to renew their vows of 40 years, ready to give my mom's eulogy, I looked up as I stood under the crucifix and was reminded of one of the powerful messages passed on by Jesus... the message to Love Your Enemy.

My mind struggled with this idea... how can I love such an evil enemy... an enemy that had put us all through so much, showing no mercy, an enemy that callously moved on to the next person after brutally ending my mom's life, without having to answer to justice. How could I love such an enemy?

But then it dawned on me... sometimes it's not what you get for what you go through... it's what you become for it.

So I stood there... following the wishes of my mom....
in the spirit of what Jesus taught... and shared the blessings of the experience with a "Thank You" to cancer...

Thank you Cancer:

For inspiring us to spend more time with the amazing woman who brought us into this world.

For helping us see the importance of slowing down and not take any day for granted.

We learned so much about mom and grew a new respect for her, her life, her spirit, not only as a great mom, but as an amazing woman.

Thank you cancer for if it had not been for you, we may have never just sat with my mom, without distraction of TV, phone, or computer. We may have never taken the time to just talk, look at pictures, talk about God, life, laugh, cry... share our victories and losses...

My brother, sister, and I would have never stepped up to consciously appreciate all our beautiful mother had done for us and our family...

We may have never taken the time to thank my mom in person, while holding her hand:

For always having a smile on her face when she picked us up from the school bus stop.

For always letting us get a lollipop after a haircut.

For getting me and my brother superhero under-roos.

For making sure I always had a good soccer ball to play with.

For always cheering us on when we were winning.

For always cheering us on when we were losing.

For protecting us even if at times it was protecting us from ourselves.

For teaching us to keep our elbows off the table and to say please and thank you.

For helping us to see that sometimes the best answer a parent can give is an observing protective silence.

For giving me a wonderful, strong, intelligent, and loving little sister.

And a big brother who will always be a hero to me.

For teaching us what unconditional love is.

For being an amazing wife and soul-mate.

For inspiring all of us with her strength and perseverance that shocked even the medical community.

Yes, cancer, by threatening death, what you did, was breathe new life into our family's relationship, our connection... our sense of unity, history, and reinforced our appreciation for the undying power of love.

Thank you cancer for inspiring everyone in my family to strengthen our bond with our wonderful mother...

and bring forward our unspoken faith in God and his perfectly imperfect order.

Cancer, God has structured the universe in such a magnificent way that even an evil force like you can only affect the impermanent... you can only kill, what in essence, was dying anyway.

But you can never touch the permanent, the love, the laughter, the victories, the family connection... you can never take away one single hug, or comforting kiss... and you can never dilute the wonderful memories and endless love we have for our mom.

Mom passed peacefully; surrounded by the people she loved so dearly.

My mom: An amazing woman whose timeless wisdom I am still discovering. She will forever be missed. She will forever be loved.

I'm not even sure why I'm sharing this story. I feel there is a message in it for the right person who reads it. Maybe it will inspire you to express your love more or live your life more daringly or maybe you're going through the same thing now with your mom or dad... I don't know. But if it helps even one person, it's worth it for me to share.

𝕾𝕺𝕼

It seems to me that religion is losing momentum and God is making a comeback.

𝕾𝕺𝕼

If I do not personify God, you call me an atheist. But I do not personify God because I refuse to limit God to the boundaries of my imagination... or yours.

𝕾𝕺𝕼

It is in the balancing of your spirituality with your humanity that you will find immeasurable happiness, success, good health, and love.

𝕾𝕺𝕼

When you pray, you are speaking to yourself. When you take action, you are speaking to God.

𝕾𝕺𝕼

Understanding the beauty of our humanity unlocks the power of our spirituality.

𝕾𝕺𝕼

Eden is within you; it is your life's garden. It is from this internal garden that you experience your external life. If you see weeds, pluck them!

𝕾𝕺𝕼

Spirituality is NOT the gauge at which we should measure our humanity.

𝕾𝕺𝕼

Notes to my Younger Self

Being healthy is a way of life. It's not just about what you feed your body; it's about what you feed your mind and the social environment you keep. Make healthy food choices, exercise your body and brain, and choose your friends wisely.

What Would Jesus Say?

During the early 90's, the Catholic Church had come under a high profile storm of anger and backlash from financial indiscretions and the horrendous discovery that the church was protecting priests that had been sexually assaulting children.

I was raised Catholic and while my personal experience of my church and its representatives was wonderful, I wrote this piece in 1994 as an act of young rebellion; I was 19. It was originally titled "I Am Here".

Dear Church,

I am here! I have never left. I am here!

Where have YOU been? When did I ever celebrate wealth? You heathen! If you are to be divinity, why do you clothe in fine clothing?

Why do you sip from the golden chalice? I am nowhere in the emptiness of greed. Why do you ask for more riches if only you build more dividers?

You are the wolf that lies to the sheep. You are no Shepherd! You slither behind my commandments while gathering riches. You speak of my Second Coming as though I had left. I am the light! I am absolute permanence! You are as impermanent as the riches you collect.

You sing the songs of the Lord so loudly that your silent evils will not be heard. You do not follow me for you do not follow what I have taught.

The sheep will soon be wise to the wolf. The wolf will perish. And my sheep will come back to me - for I have never left. I am here!

~ Jesus

The writers of religious scriptures and texts would have done humanity a grand service if they would have used just one sentence, in one of the pages out of the thousands, to support respectful and peaceful disagreement.

೮೦೦೩

Each day carries in the blessings of God and you have unlimited access to all it offers.

೮೦೦೩

Don't question your ability. You were created to succeed and live a life of purpose. Don't you dare put a question-mark where God put a period!

೮೦೦೩

I keep hearing about a spiritual awakening, but I feel what we need instead, is a human one. It would be wonderful and empowering to become free from the disillusionment and nonsense being sold to us from gurus for centuries.

೮೦೦೩

Think of the patience God has had for you and let it resonate to others. If you want a more patient world, let patience be your motto.

೮೦೦೩

If your salvation was dependent on your ability to read and understand scripture, Jesus would have been an author.

೮೦೦೩

You can speak with spiritual eloquence, pray in public, and maintain a holy appearance, but it is your behavior that will reveal your true character.

೮೦೦೩

God is the story
nature tells to
those who are
listening.

On Earth as it is in Heaven

The greatest minds, the most impactful influencers, the potent individuals whose lives have echoed long past their days; mastered the art of speaking to God without saying a word.

This wondrously vast earth is home to billions of people who speak thousands of languages. I find it to be so masterful that regardless of where you live, regardless of what language you speak, regardless of who you call God, regardless of your beliefs, and regardless of your education... the universally understood language is ACTION.

Actions speaks! Do you really want to achieve your goals? Action will say so. Do you really want to enhance your relationship? Action will say so. Do you really want to live a healthier life? Action will say so. Do you really believe in your God? Action will say so.

Action separates the heroes from the cowards, the achievers from the complainers, the successful from the mere dreamers, the happy from the envious; it separates those who rise to the challenge of their goals from the haters who cower in the shadow of inaction.

How would your life be different if you decided to speak the powerful universal language of action? If you want to change your life, waste no more time or energy with the same limp words you have used before... ACT upon it!

Your marriage, your career, your health, your family, your dreams... ACT! Be courageous enough to find yourself amongst the few people who chose to transcend the foolish dynamic of verbal philosophical creation and engage in the rare potency of well-delivered purposeful action. Speak your life into form!

> It would be ridiculous to hold your breath and blame others for your inability to breathe. In the same sense, it is ridiculous to live an unaligned life and blame God for your misfortune.

ഇരു

The world is my church. My actions are my prayer. My behavior is my creed.

ഇരു

Spirituality is the poetry of our experience. Science is the gauge of our reality. Together, they create the essence of our humanity.

ഇരു

If you would stop worrying about things you don't control and release what God has put into you, you will change everything around you.

ഇരു

The Spirituality and Self-Help industry wants you to be empowered enough to buy their products, but disempowered enough to still think you need them.

ഇരു

In moments of prayer, people tend to pose as a critic and point out perceived flaws in God's art.

ഇരു

Old religious dogma attempts to convince you that you are on a journey to God; then makes you pay tolls along the roadway.

ഇരു

No matter what the cause, God is only as willing as you are.

ഇരു

Notes to my Younger Self

Express your emotions in a multidimensional manner. Don't just speak; act! Don't just say; show!

Reflections on God

The experience of God is a subjective one; a personal awareness...

God is to be felt in your core; not to be measured with an instrument...

To argue or defend our personal experience of God is a waste of energy...

To impose our subjective experience of God on others as an objective reality is an insoluble task and a misuse of time...

If the idea of God was to be held captive by the written word, Jesus would have been an author instead of an activist...

Jesus walked ahead of his disciples and told them to "follow" him; yet with all the walking of their travels, they never arrived... it's ALL about the journey...

This practice of "following" is lost in the calling of one's self a Christian; placing Christ as your colleague... this leads to the hubristic act of judging others and losing sight of the great message... the message is best lived when one is a student of Christ... placing Jesus back in His role as Teacher... one to be followed...

No matter what your religion, the most effective way to represent it is to avoid arguing and defending the details of the story, but to faithfully live the beauty of the message...

YOU are the measure... God is most forgiving when YOU are... God is most loving when YOU are... God is most helpful when YOU are... God is most willing when YOU are... God is most accepting when YOU are... The greatness or folly of God is expressed through YOU...

Each day we are born into a new dimension of endless opportunities to be a grand expression of God; not with our words, but with our deeds...

> *Love – Acceptance – Unity – Peace – Integrity – Respect... a strong, pure creed is short on words and long on nourishing ideas. For me, the longer the creed the more it has been diluted, manipulated, and spoiled. The results of this creed poisoning can be seen in the behavior of its followers. We have all heard the expression, "The devil is in the details"; my observations have led me to suspect this is true.*

ഹര

Do not question your ability or worthiness. God is a universe of purpose -driven balance. If you have been called to action, it is because you have it within you to rise to the challenge of your calling. Now, RISE to it!

ഹര

I am so grateful for the many times God has shown me the mercy of not giving me what I want.

ഹര

God didn't give fear a body. God gave love a body.

ഹര

While spirituality provides an efficient and endless fuel for your mind and body, you must burn that fuel with human action towards your goals, dreams, and desires.

ഹര

God is not subject to religion. Religion is subject to God.

ഹര

We need more than just the Law of Attraction. We need to connect with its more successful twin, the Law of Generosity. And further entwine ourselves with their parent; the Law of Love.

ഹര

You are not on a journey
to God; you are on a
journey WITH God.

About Steve Maraboli

Steve Maraboli is a life-changing Speaker, bestselling Author, and Behavioral Science Academic. His empowering words, strategic insights, and social philosophies have been shared and published throughout the world in more than 25 languages.

Steve has delivered his inspiring, entertaining, and unforgettable speeches in over 30 countries. His quotes and videos have become a social media sensation, being shared by millions across the globe and earning him the designation of, "The most quoted man alive."

He is a Professional Contributor to numerous media outlets, including The Huffington Post, Psychology Today, Inc. Magazine, Success Magazine, and others. For over 20 years, Steve has contributed to and created empowerment, education, and humanitarian programs in over 40 countries.

He is the creator of Psycho-Neuro-Actualization™; a breakthrough counseling/coaching methodology that has gained world-wide attention for its effectiveness in influence and personal/group mindset adjustment. PNA has been called, "The Science of Influence" and "The Science of Excellence", but Steve jokingly refers to it as, "The science of getting out of your own way."

With 15+ years of successful experience as a Business Consultant, Executive/Leadership Coach, and Peak Performance Coach, Steve Maraboli works with his clients world-wide through Skype.

He is a member of:

Air Force Association
USAF Security Forces Association
Behavioral Science and Policy Association
Society for Public Health Education
Psychiatric Rehabilitation Association

One of the most quoted living writers, Steve is the author of several international bestsellers: "Life, the Truth, and Being Free", "The Power of One", and "La Vida, La Verdad, Y Ser Libre".

www.stevemaraboli.com

www.instagram.com/stevemaraboli

www.twitter.com/stevemaraboli

www.facebook.com/authorstevemaraboli

www.youtube.com/stevemaraboli

www.pinterest.com/stevemaraboli

www.linkedin.com/in/stevemaraboli

A Global Sensation – Heard and Viewed in Over 100 Countries!

Free yourself from the prison of your conditioned thoughts and destroy barriers that hinder your success.

Steve and his expert guests take you on a quest for truth and highlight philosophies and strategies that help you release your greatest self.

It's time to shake off mediocrity, destroy personal barriers, live up to your greatest potential, and align with happiness, success, and excellence.

"It's more than just a show... It's an event!"

www.empoweredlivingradio.com

Psycho-Neuro-Actualization ™
Certification Courses

Steve Maraboli now offers training and an accredited certification to professionals looking to separate themselves from the pack.

CALL TODAY to become amongst the elite professionals certified in the world's most effective system of influence!

Accredited Certification Courses for:

- Mental Health Professionals
- Personal, Professional, & Life Coaches

Professional Certification Courses for:

- Sales Professionals
- Speakers, Writers, & Influencers

www.stevemaraboli.com

A Better Today Publishing

*A Better Today Publishing is dedicated to publishing
books and media that empower, inspire, and educate.*

We are a proud part of the A Better Today family!

Visit us at: **www.abettertodaypublishing.com**

For more information please contact us at:

**A Better Today Publishing
P.O. Box 1433
Port Washington, NY 11050**

www.abettertodaypublishing.com

About A Better Today International

A Better Today International is a private philanthropic organization dedicated to creating educational, empowerment, and humanitarian programs across the globe.

Started in 1997 with just a simple website and by handing out flyers at a local train station, A Better Today International has rapidly grown and its programs and charitable works have gained international reach and recognition. Today, A Better Today International has programs running all across the USA as well as in over 40 countries world-wide.

A self-funded empowerment and humanitarian organization, A Better Today International uses its own profits to fund its programs and has volunteers that number in the thousands globally. (A Better Today Community)

Steve Maraboli and A Better Today International have received numerous awards and recognition including from 3 U.S. Presidents and the United Nations.

Made in the USA
Middletown, DE
18 April 2019